Lead with Me

A Principal's Guide to Teacher Leadership

**Gayle Moller
and Anita Pankake**

EYE ON EDUCATION

EYE ON EDUCATION
6 DEPOT WAY WEST, SUITE 106
LARCHMONT, NY 10538
(914) 833–0551
(914) 833–0761 fax
www.eyeoneducation.com

Library of Congress Cataloging-in-Publication Data

Moller, Gayle.
    Lead with me : a principal's guide to teacher leadership / by Gayle Moller & Anita Pankake.
       p. cm.
    Includes bibliographical references and index.
ISBN 1-59667-025-8
1. Teacher participation in administration. 2. Teacher-principal relationships. 3. Educational leadership. I. Pankake, Anita M., 1947- . II. Title.
LB2806.45.M65 2006
371.1'06—dc22

                                                  2006003007

10 9 8 7 6 5 4 3 2

Editorial and production services provided by
Richard H. Adin Freelance Editorial Services
52 Oakwood Blvd., Poughkeepsie, NY 12603-4112
(845-471-3566)

Also Available from EYE ON EDUCATION

What Great Principals Do *Differently*:
15 Things That Matter Most
Todd Whitaker

What Successful Principals Do!
169 Tips for Principals
Franzy Fleck

Smart, Fast, Efficient:
The New Principals' Guide to Success
Leanna Stohr Isaacson

BRAVO Principal!
Sandra Harris

The Administrator's Guide
to School Community Relations, 2nd Ed.
George E. Pawlas

School Leader Internship: Developing, Monitoring,
and Evaluating Your Leadership Experience, 2nd Ed.
Martin, Wright, Danzig, Flanary, and Brown

Talk It Out!
The Educator's Guide to Successful Difficult Conversations
Barbara E. Sanderson

Making the Right Decisions: A Guide for School Leaders
Douglas J. Fiore and Chip Joseph

Dealing with Difficult Teachers, 2nd Ed.
Todd Whitaker

Dealing with Difficult Parents
And with Parents in Difficult Situations
Todd Whitaker and Douglas Fiore

20 Strategies for Collaborative School Leaders
Jane Clark Lindle

Great Quotes for Great Educators
Todd Whitaker and Dale Lumpa

Elevating Student Voice:
How To Enhance Participation, Citizenship, and Leadership
Nelson Beaudoin

Stepping Outside Your Comfort Zone:
Lessons for School Leaders
Nelson Beaudoin

What Great Teachers Do *Differently*:
14 Things That Matter Most
Todd Whitaker

Motivating & Inspiring Teachers
The Educational Leader's Guide for Building Staff Morale
Todd Whitaker, Beth Whitaker, and Dale Lumpa

The Principal as Instructional Leader:
A Handbook for Supervisors
Sally J. Zepeda

Instructional Leadership for School Improvement
Sally J. Zepeda

Six Types of Teachers:
Recruiting, Retaining, and Mentoring the Best
Douglas J. Fiore and Todd Whitaker

Supervision Across the Content Areas
Sally J. Zepeda and R. Stewart Mayers

The ISLLC Standards in Action:
A Principal's Handbook
Carol Engler

Harnessing the Power of Resistance:
A Guide for Educators
Jared Scherz

Data Analysis for Continuous School Improvement
Victoria L. Bernhardt

Handbook on Teacher Evaluation:
Assessing and Improving Performance
James Stronge & Pamela Tucker

About the Authors

Gayle Moller is associate professor in the Department of Educational Leadership and Foundations at Western Carolina University in Cullowhee, North Carolina. She was formerly executive director of the South Florida Center for Educational Leaders. The center served large, urban school systems in South Florida that provided staff development for school leaders. Gayle worked in the Broward County Public Schools (Ft. Lauderdale, Florida) for 19 years as a teacher, school administrator, and staff development administrator. Gayle received her doctorate from Teachers College at Columbia University. Teacher leadership and professional learning communities are her research interests. Gayle served on the Board of Trustees of the National Staff Development Council. She is a coauthor, with Marilyn Katzenmeyer, of *Awakening the Sleeping Giant: Helping Teachers Develop as Leaders* (2nd edition). Gayle and her husband, Jim, live in Franklin, North Carolina.

Anita M. Pankake, a former teacher, team leader, assistant principal, and principal, is currently director of the doctoral program and professor of educational leadership at the University of Texas Pan American. Anita holds an undergraduate and master's degree from Indiana State University in Terre Haute, Indiana, and her doctorate from Loyola University in Chicago. She authored *Implementation: Making Things Happen* (1998) and coauthored *The Effective Elementary Principal* (1991). In addition, she is coeditor of three books, the most recent being *Administration and Supervision of Special Instructional Programs* (2nd edition). She is an active member of the National Staff Development Council. She serves as president of the Texas Staff Development Council and is a past president of the Texas Council of Women School Executives. Anita and her husband, David, live in Edinburg, Texas.

Acknowledgments

As in any endeavor like writing a book, there are colleagues, friends, and family members who deserve our sincere appreciation for their patience and continuing encouragement of our work. First, we would like to acknowledge the support of our professional colleagues at our respective universities, Western Carolina University and the University of Texas Pan American. Significant contributions to this book are quotes from accomplished teacher leaders who are members of the Teacher Leaders Network (TLN; http://www.teacherleaders.org), sponsored by the Center for Teaching Quality (CTQ) in Chapel Hill, North Carolina. We are indebted to Barnett Berry, President, and John Norton, Communications Advisor, who generously allowed us to lurk on the TLN daily discussion to learn from these teacher leaders and then helped us to obtain the teachers' permission to use their words in our work. We would like to further acknowledge and thank John Norton for his permission to use principal diary excerpts from MiddleWeb (http://www.middleweb.com). We treasure our personal friends who encouraged us during the process, including D'Ette Cowan, Jane Huffman, Kris Hipp, Marilyn Katzenmeyer, and Dianne Olivier. Our graphic representation of the Intentional Leadership Model took form with the technical talents of Ramiro Lazano and Angelo Morsello. In addition, Robin Hitch pulled the final product together with her masterful word processing skills. There is a special "thank you" to Bob Sickles, our publisher, who remained positive regardless of the number of times we promised a final manuscript. Most important, though, is our heartfelt gratitude for the support of our husbands, Jim Moller and David Pankake, who waited patiently on the sidelines while we were consumed with this work. Jim and David are our best friends and truly gifted educators.

Foreword

A few years ago I visited a Florida middle school to meet and talk with the principal. I was in for a surprise.

I arrived at the office and asked the secretary the whereabouts of the school's leader. He was in the library at a faculty meeting. I joined the meeting-in-progress and stood unobtrusively at the back of the room where a lively discussion was in progress, relating the curriculum of each grade to that of the other grades. The surprise wasn't that the group was wrestling so successfully with this consequential, often contentious, matter in a forthright, thoughtful, even cordial way. The surprise was that more than an hour passed before it became clear which of these educators was the principal!

That scene has always provided for me a vivid working definition of "teacher leadership."

The volume you are about to encounter is not about that remarkable school. It *is* about the nature of the crucial relationship between faculty and principal that must exist in order for teacher leadership to flourish in a school. It is about the principal relinquishing control. It is about what else a principal does that enables teachers to take responsibility for the important matters within their schoolhouse. It is about the host of impediments that teachers must overcome in order to see themselves and be seen by others as leaders. It is about why some teachers choose to have a positive influence upon the larger school as well as within their individual classrooms. And why some do not. And it is about just why a culture of shared leadership is so vital to principal, teachers, and to the learning of youngsters.

Teacher Leadership. Shared Leadership. Distributed Leadership. By whatever name we call it, the concept of a school as a community of leaders is an idea whose time has come. Why?

Dependency Training: If the John Wayne or Joan of Arc school of heroic, solitary leadership ever existed, it no longer does. Schools are much too complex and demanding places and have way too many needs for any one person to address them all. I wish that more principals could recognize what one wisely confided to me: "The more adept I get at solving the problems of this school the weaker the school becomes." The true mark of the leader is not how many followers one begats but how many leaders!

An Overabundance of Underutilized Talent: Teachers are rightly demanding these days to be treated as professionals, invited to sit at the table with grownups where they can bring their abundant strengths to decisions that will affect them and their students.

Leadership and Learning: The most powerful learning for all of us comes when we don't know how to do it, we want to know how to do it, and how we do it will affect the lives of many others who depend upon us. With leadership comes learning. The teacher who leads—who assumes responsibility for the new computer center, for overseeing parental involvement, or for the science curriculum—is the teacher who is an insatiable learner.

School Reform: I have just finished reading a book whose authors studied many successful and unsuccessful attempts at school improvement. A major conclusion: "Schools that made the greatest progress in reform were democratic; they cultivated strong distributed leadership. In each of the schools we studied, school improvement was more likely to occur when key leadership tasks were performed by multiple actors in the school community, especially teachers."

Leadership Succession: Principals of even high performing schools will leave one day. All too many schools thereupon revert to low performing ways—unless a cadre of leaders from within the schools is prepared to take over. Henrick Ibsen put it best: "A community is like a ship. Everyone must be prepared to take the helm."

Pupil Achievement: And, finally, of course, there is lots of evidence of the strong relationship between a school culture hospitable to teacher leadership and to student accomplishment. For instance, a Rand Corporation study of 1000 schools concluded: "In high-performing schools (low discipline, high pupil achievement) decision making and leadership are significantly more democratic. The teachers are more involved and influential in establishing discipline, with selecting text books, designing curriculum, and even choosing their colleagues than are teachers in low performing schools."

These are among the compelling reasons I have found teacher leadership to be so vital to the health of our profession and to our illusive goal of promoting profound levels of learning among students and their educators.

James McGregor Burns, a prolific writer about leadership, once observed that "Leadership is one of the most discussed and least understood phenomenon on earth." The words that follow have made teacher leadership for me a *most* understood phenomenon. I am confident they will prove valuable to you as well.

Roland S. Barth

Table of Contents

About This Book

This book is designed to assist hard-working principals who want to see improvement in student learning, believe that teachers can be their partners in this goal, and are willing to put aside the traditional leadership of the past to move toward a new way of leading. These are the courageous principals who want to build trust among the adults so that all teachers can be involved in making decisions about teacher and student learning. We know where the support for changes in a school must be; while principals may not always be the sources of change, they most certainly are essential advocates. If principals can be supported in their work to lead in a new way, there is the likelihood that school change will start, grow, and stay over time.

This book is organized in a way that recognizes the busy lives of principals who must snatch opportunities for their own professional renewal while dealing with intruding school issues. To help the reader, we purposefully built in repetition of ideas throughout the book. Our belief is that returning to the key ideas in our framework enhances the possibility that the reader will understand the connections between chapters. It also allows the chapters to be read out of sequence without losing the big picture.

The division of the book into three parts was not arbitrary, but designed to make the book user-friendly. Certainly our first choice would be for every reader to start at the beginning and read through the entire book. However, the organization allows for other methods. We believe that it is essential for everyone to read Part 1, which contains the foundational information on which the remaining chapters are built. In Chapter 1, readers will explore the principles on which the suggested practices that follow are based. Chapter 2 starts out with a description of Markham Middle School, where teacher leadership is well-developed and influences the core operations of the school. Following the school vignette, teacher leadership is defined, characteristics of teacher leaders are described, and a list of reasons for building and sustaining teacher leadership is shared. Chapter 3 includes information about the change process and readiness strategies that are requisite for moving toward fully implementing this new way of leading and learning.

The three chapters in Part 2 focus on the principles that form the framework for the book: building positive relationships, distributing power and authority, and aligning teacher leadership and teacher learning. In this part of the book, readers may choose to read the chapters in sequence or select the most relevant for their situation.

Part 3 focuses on principal actions needed to assure the ongoing development of teacher leadership. In Chapter 7 we address the special needs of teacher leaders with regard to their own learning, including leadership skills that may not have been a part of their professional preparation. Additionally, this chapter emphasizes the special relationships that must develop between principals and teacher leaders. Characteristics of these relationships include mutual trust, mentoring, and accountability. Chapter 8 revisits Markham Middle School, seven years later, as the development of teacher leadership continues not only at the school but throughout the school system. We briefly describe what we believe to be important actions that should be taken to assure that teacher leadership continues to function as a key component of achieving the school's vision of student learning, even in the face of formal leadership changes and other predictable disruptors. This last chapter ends with a letter from Jay, the principal of Markham Middle School, challenging other principals to usher in this new way of leading and learning.

Throughout the book, to strengthen ideas and recommendations, we draw on teacher leader and principal voices through direct quotes that are set  off in shaded boxes. We believe that these messages from people who lead in a new way and from acknowledged teacher leaders who desire to work in this type of school culture will remind the reader about the importance of this work. In addition, in most chapters we provide resources and practical tools that can be used by school leaders. When there is a resource or an applicable tool provided at the end of the chapter, icons are placed in the text to alert the reader.

Resource   Tool

Our hats are off to those courageous principals and other leaders who will embrace the ideas in this book. Their efforts and their willingness to put these ideas into action will enrich schools with increased learning for both adults and students.

Gayle & Anita

Part 1

Taking Responsibility for Intentional Leadership

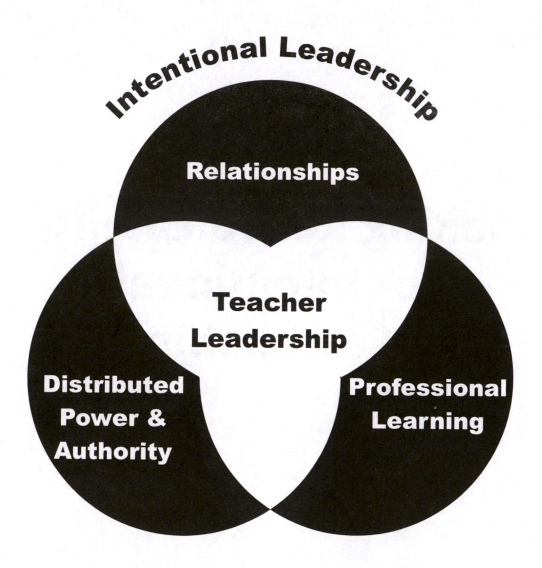

Part 1

Taking Responsibility for Intentional Leadership

The Framework for Intentional Leadership, located on the opposite page, is a graphic interpretation of the principal leadership promoted in this book. Within the figure are circles that represent the principles on which this work is based: building positive relationships, distributing power and authority, and aligning teacher leadership and professional learning. When successful implementation of these three conditions converges, teacher leadership emerges and thrives, as denoted in the overlap of the three circles. However, none of this will happen without the principal's purposeful actions in each of the three inner circles; therefore, intentional leadership is on the outside of the graphic, representing how it drives the development of teacher leadership.

Part 1 consists of three chapters that provide the knowledge base needed to make the best use of the recommended actions proposed in the parts that follow. In Chapter 1, "Ushering in a New View of Leading and Learning," the rationale for the Framework for Intentional Leadership is presented. In Chapter 2, "Investigating the Vision, the Roles, and the Reasons," a vignette describing a school where teacher leadership is well developed clarifies the vision. This is followed by definitions of teacher leadership and descriptions of those who emerge as teacher leaders, the roles they take, and the benefits of teacher leadership to individual teachers, the school, and the principal. Chapter 3, "Developing a Culture of Continuous Improvement," provides an overview of how complex it is to introduce change in a school culture due to the diversity of individual teacher's reactions to proposed changes. The principal is offered interventions to consider when dealing with this diversity.

1

Ushering in a New View of Leading and Learning

In most schools, the principal is the person at the top of the hierarchy who directs and evaluates the work of the faculty and staff in all facets of its mission. In the past, the principal was responsible for management responsibilities, maintaining order, hiring teachers, working with the community, and addressing any other unanticipated problems that only the principal could resolve. These expectations still exist, but there are the added burdens of high-stakes testing, increased numbers of special interest groups, expanded regulations, and heightened parent demands. Additionally, the principal must be the liaison for school system demands, the instructional leader, and an innovator in operations. Every element of the organization appears to be dependent on the strengths and talents of this single individual. Most principals struggle to meet these ever-expanding expectations. Unfortunately, many leave the position, resulting in recurring turnover and a shortage of highly qualified principals who are not being replaced because teacher leaders recognize the undesirability of these administrative roles.

It would seem then, that the time has come for a change in the way we structure school leadership. The present structure is not working effectively for principals, teachers, or students. Rather than trying to do it all, principals should follow the precept that "good principals are more hero-makers than heroes" (Barth, 2001, p. 448). We believe that principals can intentionally support these "heroes," or teacher leaders, to move schools beyond the current leadership quandary if they view leadership as more than just a few people in formal roles.

This new leadership structure emerges within a community of learners focused on the moral purpose of schooling—improved student learning. A principal's attention to this work could certainly be grounded in a variety of goals, such as reducing the work overload or preventing chaotic interactions, but the most important reason is to ensure a sustained focus on the school's vision for student learning. The improvement of teaching and learning in schools cannot be left to chance, so principals' actions must endeavor to meet this goal. Whatever the motive for seeking the principalship, the primary responsibility, once in the position, should be providing leadership that builds an ongoing commitment to continuous improvement of teaching that results in improved learning for all students.

In this chapter, we explore the expanding instructional leadership responsibilities of principals and discuss how teacher leaders are essential to success in achieving accountability for all students' learning. Then we present the three principles that support a framework for principals' actions. Finally, we put forward the major premise of the book: principals can learn how to be intentional in their leadership in order to promote, build, and sustain teacher leading and learning.

Shifting Scope of Principal Responsibilities

The main difference between highly effective and less effective principals is that the former are actively involved in curricular and instructional issues and the latter spend most of their time on organizational maintenance and student discipline (Cotton, 2003). Principals can become consumed with issues not directly related to instruction, but to be successful, they must make students' learning needs the top priority. This alone makes it imperative that principals take this responsibility seriously.

From the Field Someone I had known as a teacher became an administrator. Advice given to him by someone else who had already made that change was, "Now you've had the last honest conversation with a teacher. You can't talk to them the same way any longer."

Carolyn Guthrie, NBCT Teacher
TLN Member
Miami-Dade County Public Schools, Florida

Historically, the evolution of the administrative role moved the principal into responsibilities that provide indirect support to the teaching and learning process. One consequence of this is the lack of opportunities for principals and teachers to work together, often resulting in adversarial roles. Now, with the increased emphasis on accountability for student learning, bridges must be built between the administrative and the instructional functions. Effective principals and teacher leaders are the pioneers in these developing but fragile relationships.

Principal leadership and teacher leadership can be represented by Venn diagrams. When there is little or no overlap between teacher leadership and principal leadership, the two circles of the diagram barely touch (Figure 1.1),

Figure 1.1. No Interdependence

indicating that the classroom activities and school operations are functioning but there is no overlap between the two entities—principals manage schoolwide issues, and teachers take care of their individual classrooms. This situation often occurs when well-meaning principals try to protect the teachers' time by doing as much as possible alone so that teachers are not burdened. It also happens when principals do not know how to collaborate or fear the risk inherent in these interactions.

Figure 1.2. Beginning Stages of Interdependence

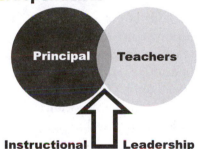

When principals increase their time spent on instructional activities and teachers participate in leadership responsibilities, the two circles begin to overlap (Figure 1.2), indicating that the faculty are beginning to view instructional and management issues as closely related. Teachers' classroom leadership experiences may bring an important perspective to the decisions and activities being initiated at the school level. As success with in-

Figure 1.3. Principal and Teacher Leadership Interdependence

dividual projects and processes reveals the positive impact that teacher leadership can have, and as schoolwide issues and programs are moved into classrooms, the amount of coordination and collaboration between teacher leaders and principals will continue to increase. When fully implemented, a range of 30 to 50 percent overlap of the two entities—administrative leadership and teacher leadership—exists (Figure 1.3). More than 50 percent overlap might intrude on the teachers' energy and time needed to focus on their fundamental work of instructing students.

Since principals must address both day-to-day demands and provide leadership for instructional improvement, they are faced with three options:

- *Do everything themselves or with a few teachers they select.* The impracticality of doing everything alone becomes more evident as the principal's responsibilities expand. Working with a few teachers establishes elitism or creates the illusion that there are "insiders" who influence the principal, thus discouraging other teachers who might lead.

- *Sit back and let leadership occur in a chaotic manner.* Letting leadership emerge haphazardly may result in dysfunctional teacher leadership, creating a toxic school culture.

- *Intentionally plan and facilitate the process of collaborative leadership.* Effective principals choose to be intentional and skilled in their efforts to build collaborative leadership. Since teacher leaders will influence others one way or another, we advocate that principals ensure that teacher leadership is focused on student learning.

We suggest that principals not hold "leadership rights," but be responsible for creating opportunities for teachers to lead and learn. This is not a quick-fix program; instead, developing teacher leadership demands high energy and devoted time over an extended period. None of this happens unless the formal leader, the principal, is *intentional* about facilitating the effort. In the following section we describe three related principles that, coupled with the principal's intent, can result in effective teacher leadership.

Principles for Promoting, Building, and Sustaining Quality Teacher Leadership

The guiding principles in this section provide the framework for this book. Building positive relationships, distributing power and authority, and aligning teacher leadership with teacher learning focus the principal's actions on increased teacher leading and learning.

Principle #1: Leadership Through Relationships

To promote, build, and sustain quality teacher leadership, positive relationships are essential. The relationships become the primary determiner of how effective a principal will be. Donaldson (2001) states that "leadership is a *relational,* not an individual phenomenon" (pp. 5–6). Principals have the formal power and authority to lead a school, but their effectiveness as leaders depends on the willingness of the people to follow. Leadership can surface in unpredictable ways. There are many principals who have the false impression that they are leading, when, in fact, powerful teachers with social networks operate more effectively to spread their influence throughout the school, often producing undesirable results. Principals may blame teacher cliques, the "old guard," or community politics. Principals learn about these relationship landmines from on-the-job experience. Moreover, they have learned in graduate courses about the legal, ethical, and fiscal responsibilities of the principal. It does not take long for new and potential principals to realize it takes courage to share leadership. As a result, many principals retreat from building these relationships, thus preventing schools from moving toward a new model of leadership.

Lambert (2002) suggests "that leadership is beyond person and role and embedded in the patterns of relationships" (p. 42). Channeling this leadership depends on the principal's ability to build relationships both inside and outside the school. The principal acknowledges negative leadership structures, builds on existing positive leadership networks, establishes new leadership structures, and, possibly, dismantles dysfunctional groups in order to move the school toward a shared vision focused on student learning.

If the principal is committed to this different, perhaps new, concept of leadership, then the real work begins, because many teachers are reluctant to take on leadership responsibilities. These teachers may not have the self-confidence to take on leadership roles, or they may be hesitant based on previous leadership experiences where they felt manipulated or not supported. Thus, principals may need to extend invitations more than once before trust is developed and the teachers believe they will have the necessary power and authority to lead. In other cases, teachers may be reluctant because they do not see leadership roles connected to what they care about in their work. Regardless of the reasons teachers hesitate to lead or the strategies used to encourage leadership, the best predictor of success for engaging teachers in leadership activity is the strength of the positive relationships between the principal and the teachers (Smylie & Brownlee-Conyers, 1992).

The essence of teacher leadership is relationships—administrator to teacher, teacher to teacher, teacher to student, administrator and teacher to community. No other responsibility is more difficult for a principal than balancing existing, new, and potential adult relationships. As teacher leaders seek to influence other teachers, they will depend on the principal to help safeguard their relationships with those they hope to influence.

Positive relationships are the foundation on which principals gain confidence to distribute power and authority. The risks that principals fear in letting go of their formal control of decisions are most frequently based on the actual or perceived tenuous relationships throughout the school.

Principle #2: Leadership Requires Distributed Power and Authority

From the Field Those who teach in supportive, innovative schools invariably have a great administrator somewhere—and it can all go away in a heartbeat.

Nancy Flanagan
NBCT Music Teacher
TLN Member
Hartland, Michigan

To promote, build, and sustain quality teacher leadership requires authentic distribution of power and authority. The high-energy, unusually talented principal may seem ideal for a school; however, principals with these characteristics are exceptions, if they exist at all. In reality, principals should not strive to meet the expectations for a charismatic leader. Collins (2001), in his study of companies with long-term high performance, found that charismatic leaders were a liability for sustaining improvement. After the principal leaves, if there is not a critical mass of teacher leaders to continue the improvement efforts, the change usually dissolves.

To change from the single-leader model requires the distribution of power and authority. Principals have authority vested by school system policies, and by virtue of this authority, they have power. Principals who view their power and authority as tools for expanding leadership are at the forefront in leading today's schools. The principal must move from retaining power *over* others, which is based on rules, to giving power *to* others, which is goal directed (Sergiovanni, 2000). These principals know that their own power can expand if they share it. Taking action on the belief that distributing power can lead to more effective organizational results is risky, but it can result in unlimited opportunities for the school.

Teachers, however, cannot be empowered in the absence of opportunity to accept and exercise that power. The majority of teachers want to do what is best for students, and it is easier to do this when they work in a supportive culture. Therefore, the principal's role is to develop a school culture where teachers are authentically engaged in leadership and where diverse perspectives are welcomed. This is another reason to move away from the hero leader—to build a democratic school community. The curriculum standards require teachers to instruct students about democracy, but students see that teachers do not have a role in school decision making, and, in turn, many teachers do not offer students opportunities to make decisions in their classrooms. In addition, teachers are asked to build inclusive classrooms, but they are not included in essential decision making.

Moving to this new way of leading does not mean relinquishing responsibility. On the contrary, it requires even more attention from the principal, who must provide support for teacher leading and learning with the expectation that teachers will improve their performance and fulfill their leadership commitments. Elmore (2002) recommends that the responsibility for improved teaching practice is a reciprocal responsibility between the principal and the teachers. If principals expect changes in instruction, then they must provide opportunities for teachers to build their capacity for these changes. In turn, if principals invest in these supportive conditions, then teachers have a responsibility to use new knowledge and skills in their teaching.

The distribution of formal power and authority demands courage from the principal, who must trust that others will fulfill their responsibilities. This combined leadership of the principal and the teachers can result in changes that one person could never initiate and sustain, or even envision. A decision principals consider in developing teacher leadership is whether or not they are willing to distribute power and authority. We hope principals believe in the benefits of such distribution, but we are also aware that there may be variations in the intensity of this belief. It is likely that a few people believe this is absolutely true, while others may be a bit more conservative believing that it is possible, but risky. There are also principals who do not deny there are possibilities but demand, "Show me, and I may become a believer." We are confident that the information offered in this book coupled with a willingness to use the suggested strategies will strengthen principals' confidence and capabilities in working with teacher leaders.

> **From the Field** Administration should appreciate it (teacher leadership) once they see it is not usurping their position but is supporting the growth of student achievement. I think there will be a collective sigh of relief.
>
> *Jessica Hale*, NBCT
> Science Teacher, TLN Member
> Orlando, Florida

Working to build relationships and then creating structures to distribute power and authority are essential for professional learning to thrive. Sometimes it is difficult to know what comes first. Do teachers become accomplished as a result of participation in quality professional learning or through their activities as teacher leaders? Regardless of the impetus, teacher leading and learning are the building blocks for school reform.

Principle #3: Leadership for Professional Learning

To promote, build, and sustain quality teacher leadership, principals must align teacher leadership with professional learning. If we want teacher leadership to result in improved student learning, then the focus of the leadership must target teacher learning. Leading and learning are symbiotic. One of the most important roles of principals is to ensure that teachers and other adults, including themselves, learn how to best teach all students. The responsibility moves beyond a single teacher's classroom to collective responsibility for all students.

Changing demographics and increased pressure to ensure learning for all student populations present a steep curve in the demand for continuous teacher learning. Sykes (1999) states that "the improvement of American education relies centrally on the development of a highly qualified teacher workforce imbued with the knowledge, skills, and dispositions to encourage exceptional learning in all the nation's students" (p. xv). At no other time in the history of our profession has teacher development been in the spotlight as it is now. The good news is that we have significant knowledge about how teachers can learn to improve their work with students. The unfortunate news is that having the knowledge and using it in practice are often not the same. Even as legislators mandate quality professional development for teachers, there are too few schools or school systems where this type of professional learning exists.

The current cognitive theories advocate for a constructivist approach in which students construct their own meaning and make sense of their world. Students must have and use critical thinking skills in order to face a world that is nonlinear and unpredictable. Teachers must be better equipped to help students master these skills, and if teachers do not experience constructivist learning themselves, it will be difficult to use these strategies to teach their students.

The complexity of teaching and learning today demands the involvement of teachers in determining their learning needs based on student data within established professional learning communities where everyone can learn together. Effective teaching strategies, based on these data, must be learned and, most important, used well through job-embedded, just-in-time collective learning. To build this level of professional learning, principals shift from being in control to supporting the development of a community of learners. When this community becomes "self-organizing," there does not have to be as strong a reliance on formal leaders, such as the principal, to continue school improvement. Depending only on the principal to do this is unrealistic. Teacher leaders can initiate the discussions that move everyone toward the shared vision for student learning. Certainly, principals can begin the work, but in the long term, it is a critical mass of teacher leaders who will keep the conversations alive.

Intentional Leadership Is Required

> **From the Field** I have come to believe that the principal is the most instrumental person in education. It is leadership that determines the level at which the school embraces opportunities for students.
>
> *Michelle Pedigo*
> Middle School Principal
> MiddleWeb Diary

This book's central premise is that building positive relationships, authentically distributing power and authority, and aligning teacher leadership with teacher learning cannot happen without principals intentionally leading the process. This level of attention to leadership requires principals to provide resources, manage school operations, and support staff for the purpose of improving student learning

The Framework for Intentional Leadership (Figure 1.4) illustrates the interrelationship of the three basic principles and how they are driven by the principal's intentional leadership. Principals cannot ignore or even delegate this responsibility (at first) because as the formal leaders, their actions signal the importance and commitment to this new way of leading and learning.

Figure 1.4. Framework for Intentional Leadership

As principals consider their readiness for teacher leadership, the rubric in Figure 1.5 can be used to determine their current level of skills. Later in the book we will use this rubric in further exploration of the three principles. The hope is that principals will move from being unsure and unskilled to becoming leaders of teacher leaders.

Figure 1.5. Intentional Leadership Rubric

Quality teacher leadership requires the following principles be in place:	
Relationships: Essential positive relationships	
Unsure & Unskilled	Teachers are known to the principal and to each other; some self-selected groups are intact. Everyone is cordial, but limited in their interactions with each other.
Moving Along	Teachers' talents, skills, and interests, as well as their social networks are known to the principal; the number of purposefully established groups has increased and most teachers are participating in one or more school structures.
Leading Teacher Leaders	Teachers' talents, skills, and interests, as well as their social networks are known to the principal and to other teachers; groups are established voluntarily, by invitation, and by assignment; the principal, teacher leaders, and teachers themselves take the initiative to link individuals together in realizing the school vision.
Power & Authority: Authentic distribution of power and authority	
Unsure & Unskilled	Principal does not trust teachers to lead and be accountable. May have one or two individuals with whom issues are discussed and some projects delegated, but only with close supervision.
Moving Along	Principal is beginning to trust a select group of teacher leaders to lead and be accountable. The teacher leaders are generally those individuals in formal leadership roles in the school.
Leading Teacher Leaders	Principal has confidence that most teachers will lead and be accountable

Professional Learning: **Alignment of teacher leadership with professional learning**	
Unsure & Unskilled	Professional learning opportunities are available, but may or may not be related to the school's vision or aligned with individual teacher needs.
Moving Along	A school vision has been developed and decisions regarding professional learning evolve from the vision. Teacher leaders are directly involved in determining what many of these learning opportunities will be.
Leading Teacher Leaders	All professional learning opportunities are aligned with the school's vision and the individuals' job needs; a variety of learning formats are employed for delivery of learning; everyone in the school is involved in continuous learning. Teacher leaders have improved their leadership skills through specific professional learning opportunities.

Summary

To continue to believe that an impossible set of expectations, including instructional leadership, can be expertly accomplished by the principal alone may well be the death knell of the position itself. Principals must move from center stage to the new role of coach. Scherer (2002) contrasts the metaphors of directing a band and coaching a soccer game to explain the type of leadership needed in schools today. The coach of the soccer team has to rely on split-second decisions made by team members, rather than trying to direct every action on the field, as a band director does. It is time for principals to intentionally move from serving as the director of school actions to being a coach for teacher leaders.

This new view of leading and learning demands intentional actions by principals to build relationships, distribute power and authority, and align teacher leadership with teacher learning. Only with this commitment can schools develop the human resources necessary to address the complex learning needs of today's students. In the next chapter, we explore teacher leadership, discuss what kind of teachers take on these leadership roles, and determine how teacher leadership benefits the teacher, the school, and the principal.

2

Investigating the Vision, the Roles, and the Reasons

Teachers played a vital leadership role in the early development of our nation's schools, so there is a certain irony that accompanies the current interest in the development of teacher leaders. Fortunately, the revival of this interest is fostering long overdue attention to where the real work of the schools occurs, in the classroom, and to reconnect administrators and teachers. In this chapter we look at teacher leadership within a middle school, where the principles described in Chapter 1 are used intentionally by a principal to build a school culture that embraces change. We then look at the meaning of the term teacher leadership as an organizational quality that emerges as teachers take on a wide range of both informal and formal roles. Finally, we explore reasons why principals would lead in a new way.

Markham Middle School

Theresa is completing her master's degree, and her current course is focused on teacher leadership. On the first night of class, she could not imagine why this course was required for her degree. After all, she did not think she was a leader, and what did this have to do with her degree in middle grades education? At the end of the course, each student must share information about a school in which leadership practices helped promote teacher leadership to improve student achievement. Theresa now knows that she does not have to visit another school because her school is perfect for this report! She realizes how teacher leadership makes a difference in her school, and she is excited to write her report.

Markham Middle School (MMS) is located in a community with changing demographics. Children who are poor and/or speak languages other than English are the majority of the students in this school that once served students primarily from middle-class homes where only English was spoken. Most of the faculty members have either taught for more than 15 years or are in the first few years of their teaching experience. The school operates using a modified middle school configuration, with four teachers on most teams representing mathematics, language arts, social studies, and science. In addition, there are teachers who teach the elective subjects, physical education, and special education. Similar to schools across the country, MMS is struggling with reduced funding, increased learning expectations for a disadvantaged student population, and high-stakes accountability testing.

Theresa has taught at MMS for nearly 15 years. She would never have been able to do this report five or six years ago when the working conditions were quite different. But now, Theresa cannot think of anyone on the faculty who does not like working at the school. There is no doubt in Theresa's mind that a major reason that MMS is operating as it is today has to do with the principal, Jay Denton. When Jay came to the school five years ago, the student achievement at MMS was considered low-performing by the state's accountability standards. Given a mandate by the superintendent to improve student achievement, Jay knew this was a school where teachers worked in isolation and had few opportunities to talk about the craft of teaching. The previous principal was popular with many of the teachers because he left the teachers alone; that is, he did not interfere or otherwise raise questions about their teaching.

Jay brought an interesting combination of experiences to MMS. He came from a principalship in an elementary school, but his teaching experience was at the middle school level. These experiences gave Jay immediate credibility with the staff as a teacher and as an administrator. The important part, however, was that Jay did not leave it at that. Immediately, he gathered information and posed questions to faculty members individually and in groups about their interests, ideas, and dreams for the school. Jay was the first administrator to ask faculty about the school they wanted rather than tell them about the school he or she planned to create. While no one knew it at the time, Jay believed in building a professional learning community that relied heavily on teacher leadership. He never actually said this was his goal; he just took actions that reflected this belief.

Theresa wants to emphasize in her report the important context changes that have occurred over the last five years. All of these were changes in the way the school operated. Now everyone remembers only dimly "how things used to be," but Theresa recalls that not all changes were welcomed; in fact, some were resisted by many of the faculty at the time they were introduced. On the other hand, as Theresa reflects on the situation, these early initiatives, such as collaborative decision making, allowed other changes to occur.

When Jay first came to the school, decision making about critical issues, such as the use of time and hiring teachers, remained with him. Within the first semester, he worked with the faculty, staff, and members of the community to develop a shared vision for the school. As trust increased between the administrative team and the teachers, Jay formed and became an active member of the Leadership Team, composed of members representing the school community. The Team's first task was to decide what would be solely Jay's decisions, when they would give Jay advice, and when there would be a collective decision. This prevented misunderstandings as the team worked together. Members of the Leadership Team learned facilitation and meeting skills to be effective. Early in the development of the team, teachers participated in external training to gain these skills. Now the outgoing members of the Leadership Team provide this professional development for new members. Today, this is where other teachers bring their ideas so that the team members can help to develop and implement them. In addition to this example of representative leadership, there is an open invitation to all teachers to be involved in decision making. Faculty meetings, team level meetings, and other structures allow all teachers to be as involved as they wish.

The interactions between and among the teachers are frequent and varied in length and intensity. These interactions are not just among individuals in a grade level or subject area but throughout the school. For example, Theresa, who works with seventh grade students in language arts, collaborated with colleagues from both sixth and eighth grades to select materials for the literacy program. While the language arts teachers were the core committee members for this effort, teachers from mathematics, social studies, and science were also involved. The discussions had varied perspectives regarding what materials might provide the best content for the students. Theresa knows she learned a great deal about the connections among these content areas, and it seemed to her that the other teachers did as well.

The committee to select literacy materials was facilitated by Yolanda, the school's literacy coach, a formal teacher leader role. The central office funded this position in schools where there were student demographics similar to those at MMS. Yolanda was a natural choice for this position based on her competency in the classroom. Teachers throughout the school admired Yolanda's ability to work with the most recalcitrant students. Even before Yolanda took the position, teachers would take time during their planning periods to observe her work with students. Yolanda agreed to assume the role on the condition that she would continue to teach two classes a day. Using the same constructivist approach she used with her students, Yolanda invites teachers to find their own voices about their teaching. Rather than working in large groups, Yolanda skillfully invites teachers, either in small groups or individually, to inquire with her about their teaching. In addition, Yolanda is a member of the school system's Curriculum Council, teaches at a local university, and participates in an external network of teacher leaders who are studying literacy.

As in most schools, professional development resources are limited, and the Leadership Team members are conscientious about how these resources are used. The Professional Development Committee members use student data to decide what type of professional development would assist the staff in working more effectively with students. The format of professional development varies depending on the need of the students and the teachers. There are times when an external expert in an instructional strategy is invited to share. At other times, teams of teachers attend conferences, visit other schools, or participate in training that is relevant to the student needs. Finally, the school frequently taps into the expertise of teachers. Regardless of the approach, there is always a plan for follow-up. At times, small groups of teachers arrange student groups in such a way that one teacher is able to have time to coteach or observe in another teacher's classroom. An important element put in place for the school, as a whole, was the time for faculty to meet together. Theresa knows that most of the faculty members now take that time for granted. As she listens to other people in her graduate courses, she learns that MMS is quite different from many schools in this regard. At MMS, there is common team planning time, and Jay has been able to provide substitute teachers for individuals and groups to work together on curriculum projects. Over the years, Theresa and her colleagues have found that when additional time can be purchased it is appreciated, but if this is not possible, teachers find time to implement new strategies, talk with each other about how they are working, offer feedback, and try again.

The commitment to professional learning is reflected in Jay's participation in most of the activities. This ensures that everyone is familiar with the new approaches, shares a common language, and can both reinforce and support each other. An example of the school's approach to professional learning started in the early stages of reform at the school, when the administrators and teachers were engaged in a literacy training program sponsored by the school system. One of the powerful strategies from this program that helped develop this "make it happen" culture over the years is the sharing of student work. Theresa has been a part of faculty development efforts in which student work was archived from each classroom over a six- to nine-week period. The student work was used to focus the conversations of the teachers on what implementing the new materials or strategies was intended to do. Archiving the work was not just a way of creating a reference point for conversation and change, it was a way to see evidence of student growth and a cause for celebration.

An example of how resources are provided for teacher learning is when Jaime, a seventh grade team leader, learned about a new critical thinking strategy. He found a teacher leader from another school who knew how to use the strategy. After his team members met with this teacher, Jay allocated money to bring the teacher back to the school to coach Jaime's team members as they started using the strategy with the students. Having this resource helped the teachers feel more comfortable with what they were doing and gave credibility to the process.

Like Jaime, other teacher leaders spread their influence throughout the school. For example, through Matt's interest in the use of action research, developed during his master's degree program, he learned the value of embedding inquiry into his teaching. At first, Matt used the strategies to investigate how to best serve the students who are English Language Learners (ELL) in his classroom. Then, in casual conversations, he shared what he was discovering with colleagues on his team. The other teachers decided to join Matt and develop a program that would provide the ELL students instruction within heterogeneous groups across their team. During the next two years, the team collected data that showed how valuable the strategy was for their students. At the end of the two years, the team members presented their results to the Leadership Team and then to the whole faculty. The faculty agreed to work with Jay to develop a schedule that would provide a similar experience for all ELL students. Now there is no tracking of these students.

Faculty turnover at this school is quite low. The one exception is when teacher leaders move to another school or a central office position when they want a new challenge, usually with Jay's encouragement. For example, Matt is currently the coordinator of the ELL program at the central office. Theresa has found through conversations in her graduate courses that low attrition is not the norm in many schools. Again, in her reflections on why MMS has a low attrition rate, she has identified three ways of operating that might explain the phenomenon.

First, when new teachers come to the school, they join the school, not just a grade-level team or a content-area department, and they are expected to be responsible for the success of students beyond their own classrooms. Even many of the old-timers, like Theresa, have changed grade levels to better meet the needs of the students. At first this was disconcerting to the faculty, but it has turned out to be an essential element in the school's transformation. Also, many have taken lead roles in a variety of instructional and support projects in which faculty from all areas of the school have been involved. Second, teachers serve on the hiring committee that includes representatives from across the school. Over the years, participating in the hiring procedures has generated feelings of ownership for everyone and a willingness to ensure the success of teachers hired.

The third system in place to reduce attrition is an induction program designed for new teachers, even for those who are not new to teaching. Once a teacher is hired, they have support over a two-year period.

Theresa has served mostly as a mentor to veteran teachers new to the school. When the induction/mentoring program was first initiated, Theresa worked with a beginning teacher; she found out quickly that this was not for her. She does much better with teachers who have a background in teaching at other schools. Working with colleagues at this level allows Theresa to share the organizational aspects that an experienced teacher new to the school needs. There are other teachers who prefer to work with the beginning teachers. In fact, Theresa's colleague, Susan, has earned the nickname "Mentor Mom" for her patience with the new teachers who need help in incredibly basic ways. Susan took the lead in organizing the mentoring/induction program about four years ago. She pulled the pieces and practices for this program together in a way that allows flexibility for both mentors and the new teachers. Participating in the program is not a requirement for all veteran faculty members, but almost everyone takes part.

There are teachers who work as informal leaders through understated actions that result in remarkable changes within their own and other teachers' classrooms. For example, within the school system, MMS has the highest percentage of teachers who are certified by the National Board of Professional Teaching Standards. This trend began around six years ago with Tim, who took the risk of working through the rigorous process. In turn, after receiving his certification, he coached other teachers on the staff on how to develop a portfolio for certification. Now Tim and other certified teachers collaborate annually to coach people who are willing to go through certification.

Theresa knows that many of the students in her graduate course will not believe much of what she will share in her report. Unfortunately, these teachers work under conditions that are not as supportive of teacher leadership. As Theresa completes her report, she now realizes and admits that she is indeed a leader at MMS.

The description of Markham Middle School captures only a snapshot of how this school capitalizes on the resources from teacher leadership and represents the new view of school leadership presented in Chapter 1. Few of these instances of teacher leadership would occur without *intentional* leadership from Jay, the principal. As the Leadership Team developed, Jay worked with the faculty and staff to develop a shared vision that would guide the team members' decisions. We assume that at first Jay frequently had to remind the group that the decisions they made must be focused on the students' learning needs. Once decisions were made, he then provided the resources, structures, and support for teacher leadership. Examples of Jay's support include securing the funding to bring a teacher leader from another school to work with Jaime's team and designing a schedule to build in time for individual teachers and groups of teachers to work on curricular and instructional projects.

At MMS, *leadership is built through relationships.* Early on, Jay took the time to listen to teachers and determine what social relationship networks existed. Matt's relationships with his team members helped put the program for ELL students into place. Jaime learned about a new teaching strategy outside of the school and influenced other teachers to learn and use the strategy with their students.

It is apparent that Jay believes *leadership requires authentic distribution of power and authority,* as evidenced in the structures developed to support teacher leaders. The Leadership Team functions as a formal structure to move the school toward the shared vision. Yolanda, a formal teacher leader, has the autonomy and responsibility to work with teachers to improve instruction. Finally, teachers are involved in the hiring and induction of new teachers.

Leadership for professional learning is apparent throughout the school. There was a schoolwide connection with an external literacy initiative, and Jay was a colearner with the teachers in this project. Individual teachers like Tim influence teachers to engage in professional learning. There is a formal structure for making decisions regarding the use of resources for professional development and a mentoring program designed to help all new teachers who come to the school.

When Jay entered MMS, these positive examples of teacher leadership were not the norm, but even at this stage of development we can predict that Jay found pockets of teaching excellence as well as the problems that are typical when people work together in any organization. This school gives us a glimpse of the variety of roles teachers take in leading a school as it makes change. Now we will look at the concept of teacher leadership and discuss who teacher leaders are.

What Is Teacher Leadership?

The term "teacher leadership" is often misunderstood. This lack of clarity can lead to confusion that results in obstacles to teachers who take on leadership roles. Most people outside education, and even many educators, do not completely understand the concept of teacher leadership. The term too often brings to mind the adversarial roles in which teachers and administrators have traditionally struggled.

Fortunately, over the last 20 years, a body of knowledge about teacher leadership has emerged. After reviewing this literature, York-Barr and Duke (2004) defined teacher leadership as "the process by which teachers, individually or collectively, influence their colleagues, principals, and other members of school communities to improve teaching and learning practices with the aim of increased student learning and achievement" (pp. 287–288). This definition of teacher leadership does not identify a person or a set of characteristics; instead, it looks at leadership as an organization quality that is influenced by teachers, staff members, and others. Fullan (2005) supports this perspective by stating that "leadership (not 'leaders') is the key to the new revolution" (p. xi) in transforming schools. The principal's role in this "process" is to create a school culture in which the teachers' knowledge, interests, talents, and skills are maximized. In time, teachers come forward to take on leadership roles and responsibilities to become powerful change agents who make a difference.

Who Emerges as Teacher Leaders?

If teacher leadership is an organizational phenomenon, then the result is the surfacing of individuals who take on leadership roles in diverse situations. These successful teacher leaders exhibit *competence*, are *credible* with other teachers, and build relationships so that they are *approachable* (Katzenmeyer & Moller, 2001).

Competent and Credible

From the Field   I knew we had four strong, well-balanced literacy teachers who had been thoroughly trained in and utilized the exact strategies we wanted to see all reading teachers embrace. These four teachers were respected by their peers. It didn't take much to get the support of these literacy "movers and shakers."

Carol Stack
Middle School Principal
MiddleWeb Diary

Schlechty (1997) defines teaching as a leadership act that resides in the primary job responsibilities of the teacher. We believe that while teacher leader actions may focus on extracurricular activities or other diverse interests, the work of teachers is student learning, and teacher leaders want their efforts to contribute to this end. Many teacher leaders have expertise in teaching and learning and are able to work with diverse students so that they are motivated to learn. These are teachers who are willing to learn themselves, and to share with others.

Competent teachers are usually recognized by their colleagues as knowledgeable and skilled in their work. Therefore, not only are they competent, they are *credible* in the eyes of their colleagues. Teachers look for resources to help them survive in the complex world of teaching, and credible teacher leaders often become those resources. Within schools, there may be a silent acknowledgment that these teachers know how best to work with students. Casually glancing into these teacher leaders' classrooms, listening to their comments in meetings, and actually talking to students of these teachers are strategies other teachers employ to learn about improving their teaching. In an isolated profession in which there is rarely time to talk about their practice, teachers must use these resources. Even if there is time, the school culture may inhibit such conversations. Regardless of how teachers determine the competence of other teachers and attribute credibility to these leaders, they do it. They intuitively know who is worthy of their confidence regarding instructional issues.

Approachable

Teacher leaders are *approachable.* They understand the importance of nurturing collaborative and trusting relationships because they are aware of the social and political structures within the teaching culture. To accomplish their work, teacher leaders establish social networks in which they have influence. Teachers who are approachable are physically present so that other teachers know how to find these leaders. They are visible in the library, the administrative offices, and in other teachers' classrooms. When a problem arises, the classroom of a teacher leader can become a haven for helping others and sharing dilemmas.

The ability to influence other teachers to improve their practice, whether by design or by chance, depends on how teachers view each other in terms of their competence, credibility, and approachability. In most cases, this process is informal, resulting from teachers learning together in work sessions, in the hallway, or as they eat lunch together. This leadership shows up in a variety of informal and formal roles.

What Are Teacher Leader Roles?

Silva, Gimbert, and Nolan (2000) describe three waves of teacher leadership roles that emerged during the recent school reform efforts. First, formal leadership roles, such as department chairperson, master teacher, or a similar position designed to maintain "an efficient and effective educational system" (p. 3) were established. Next, teachers became involved in positions that were more closely aligned with teaching and learning, such as curriculum developer or staff developer, but were primarily based outside of the classroom. Finally, the "third wave" recognized teachers as leaders within the day-to-day work of teaching. These classroom-based teachers did not have special titles, but they were working in collaboration with their colleagues to improve student learning. We believe that the teacher leadership described in each "wave" serves a purpose, depending on the context of the school.

In the real life of schools and school systems, teacher leadership emerges in a multitude of roles, each of which can provide a valuable service. Rarely, though, are all teachers willing to collaborate and formally or informally lead within a professional learning community, even with the best resources and support. Rather than advocating for specific roles for teacher leaders, we need to seek teacher leadership that best supports the improvement of teaching and learning; this may vary from school to school. For example, if a principal works in a school in which there is a history of low student performance, there may be a need for a formal lead teacher to collaborate with classroom teachers to change instructional strategies. In another school, such a formal lead teacher may inhibit collaboration among teachers, and the best approach would be to build on existing team collaboration. A single role description for teacher leaders is futile; there must be flexibility depending on the situation.

Figure 2.1 illustrates the different roles of teacher leadership. A teacher leader may work as an individual in a formal position, such as Yolanda, the literacy coach at Markham Middle School. There are situations when a formal leadership role may be necessary to move a school toward a student-learning goal. In contrast, there are individual informal leaders who are equally powerful in their influence, such as Matt, who used an instructional strategy to help his ELL students and then influenced his team members to try a program to work with these students. Teacher leaders also work in community with others, like Jaime, a formal team leader, who learned with his team members. Then there are informal teacher leaders who work in community as leaders, such as Tim, who took an interest in helping other teachers at MMS gain national certification. These examples demonstrate that there is need for diverse leadership roles at different times, and although this leadership may come primarily from the teachers, it may also emerge from the students, the staff, or the parents.

Figure 2.1. Teacher Leadership Roles

	Formal Teacher Leadership	*Informal Teacher Leadership*
Individual	Serve in the established position of literacy coach (Yolanda)	Use an instructional strategy in own classroom before influencing team members (Matt)
In Community	Serve as team leader (Jaime)	Mentor colleagues (Tim)

To better understand teacher leader roles, the next section provides concrete examples. Principals who capitalize on teacher leadership accept both informal and formal teacher leader roles as equal in importance regarding their influence, even though they are quite different in makeup and responsibilities.

Informal Teacher Leader Roles

We start with informal teacher leader roles because we believe that the most powerful influence for improved teaching and learning often comes from informal teacher leadership. In fact, when teachers are asked to identify teacher leaders based on who is *competent, credible,* and *approachable,* they frequently name those teachers in the school who do not have formal roles or titles. Whitaker (1995) found in his study of effective middle school administrators that these principals were able to identify key teacher leaders and involve them in the school's change process, whereas "less effective principals in the study were unable to recognize their informal teacher leaders" (p. 77).

Informal teacher leaders fulfill such a variety of roles that it is difficult to group them into categories. The driving force behind these committed individuals is that they have a passion for whatever issue they are addressing. Their energies may be focused on a teaching and learning issue, a student activity, or even a facility problem. These informal leaders usually see a problem, identify how to solve it, and rally the needed resources to make it happen. In addition, informal leaders are available for other teachers when they most need help for both professional and personal issues.

Later, we discuss how to identify informal leaders and build a network to take advantage of their talents. The principal's tasks are first to understand that informal teacher leadership is powerful and then to discover how to incorporate this leadership into a productive system.

Formal Teacher Leader Roles

Teachers assume formal leadership roles in community with other teachers through selection by leaders either at the school site or the central office. In contrast, there are teachers who provide formal teacher leadership as individuals through their ability to reach beyond their schools to find the professional learning or recognition they do not find locally.

Formal Teacher Leaders in Community

There are myriad ways teachers emerge as formal leaders when schools and school systems reach out to talented teachers to help reduce the gaps in student learning. In these formal teacher leadership roles, teachers work collaboratively with other teachers as school reform leaders, district or school-site resource teachers, and the more traditional managerial/leadership roles.

Teachers Selected to Be School Reform Leaders

There are many national, state, and local school reform programs in which outstanding teachers are selected to participate in intensive, long-term professional learning experiences with the expectation that they will use the new knowledge and skills and then help other teachers at the school site or within the school system learn. For example, with the infusion of funds for science and mathematics education, there are several national and state programs where teacher leaders study with scientists or mathematicians so that they gain deep knowledge in their content area. There are also literacy programs that help teachers develop in-depth knowledge of writing or reading so that they can provide quality teaching in these areas. As teachers use the literacy skills or apply their new content-area knowledge, the program directors identify leaders who can learn how to teach and coach other teachers. In time, a critical mass of teacher leaders form a cadre from which schools or school systems can draw for expertise. These teacher leaders may participate in leadership development activities in order to prepare them to work with other teachers.

District or School-Site Resource Teachers

Based on student needs data, a school or school system may determine that teacher leaders are required to work with other teachers in formal instructional leadership roles. These teachers work at a school site or with several schools to provide support in various ways, such as facilitating professional learning activities, modeling effective teaching strategies, and coaching other teachers. The titles assigned to these teachers may include lead teacher, staff developer, literacy facilitator, coach, technology specialist, or assignment to include classroom responsibilities. The advantage of a school-site position is that the teacher works within the context of the school and can adapt to its culture, whereas district resource teachers may be spread among so many schools they are unable to provide this level of service.

Managerial/Leadership Roles

Traditionally, people thought of teacher leaders as serving in roles such as department chairperson, team leader, athletic director, or school improvement team chairperson. These roles are still crucial to the effective operation of the school, and in many cases, these teacher leaders provide leadership in instruction as well as the day-to-day operational functions. Principals can enlist these leaders to work in vertical teams to address schoolwide issues.

Individual Formal Teacher Leaders

There are teachers who want to learn continuously but work in a school culture that does not support their growth and development, so they seek out their own professional learning experiences. The advantages for the school in capitalizing on these teachers' talents are obvious, and principals are in a position to identify opportunities to engage such individuals in collaboration with their peers. Regrettably, when teachers succeed in their efforts to learn, schools and school systems frequently do not tap into their leadership potential for a variety of reasons. Principals may be so busy that they do not realize that teachers have taken on this additional responsibility for their own learning, or they may not understand the level of accomplishment the teachers achieve and therefore cannot link others to this resource for learning. School leaders may also hesitate to invite these teachers to contribute because they may be unduly concerned about the negative responses from other teachers.

Teachers Who Seek Professional Learning

Teacher leaders may find it difficult to identify like-minded teachers in their schools. This may be the result of a lack of opportunities to work with other teachers in their schools, or there may not be teachers in their teaching areas that are as passionate about their work. Regardless of the reasons, national and state organizations have developed teacher leader networks in which teacher leaders can find colleagues who want to pursue conversations or study in their field of interest. These networks form around content areas, school reform issues, and even teacher leadership.

See Resources 2.1–2.7 Page 37.

Teacher Awards/Certification

There are numerous teaching awards for which teachers can self-nominate or be nominated by others, such as teacher of the year. Also, the National Board of Professional Teaching Standards supports a rigorous national certification process. When teachers are involved in applying for awards or certification, they are engaged in professional learning situations.

Today we have more highly qualified teachers than at any other time in our profession, and most are not being fully utilized as resources for solving the significant problems in our schools. The Institute for Educational Leadership Task Force on Teacher Leadership (2001) states the issue succinctly:

> [I]t is not too late for education's policymakers to exploit a potentially splendid resource for leadership and reform that is now being squandered: the experience, ideas, and capacity to lead of the nation's schoolteachers. (p. 2)

From the Field   A school system plows a lot of resources into hiring really good classroom teachers. Then they support the certification process so those teachers can become exemplary teachers…. It's great, but what are they going to do with it? It's like discovering that the ornamental blooming cherry tree you purchased for your yard has suddenly produced bushels of fruit. Exactly what are you suppose to do with all those cherries?…

Susan Graham, NBCT
Family and Consumer Science
TLN Member
Gayle Middle School
Fredericksburg, Virginia

There are thousands of teachers who are nationally certified and others who are involved in leadership roles within school reform efforts, often external to the school. Schools and school systems are investing significant resources in placing teachers in these roles. Teacher leaders are participating in national networks such as the National Writing Project, where teacher leaders learn from each other. Even with all these formal efforts to build professionalism into teaching, the engagement of teachers as leaders is absent in most schools.

Why Is Teacher Leadership Essential?

One of the most important elements affecting the acceptance of a new way of leading is a perceived need for the change. Principals have to believe that staying where they are in their practice is more painful than adopting something new, because most of us do not change unless we can see the benefits or "what's in it for me." Most of us pursue only those things we perceive as benefiting us by bringing us recognition, helping us to succeed, or aiding us in keeping our jobs or getting a better one.

We identified reasons for putting effort into the development of teacher leadership. These benefits from teacher leadership are divided into three categories. First, there are reasons specifically connected to individual teachers and teaching. Second, there are advantages for the school as a whole. Finally, principals will reap benefits related to their role.

Individual Teachers and Their Teaching

Increase Student Learning

The private act of teaching, a norm in most schools, allows inequity in instruction to be a veiled secret. The student assessment results from one teacher can be dramatically different from another teacher's students, as illustrated in Figure 2.2. Although there are variables, such as student placement, that affect these results, the data suggest that some students are learning more when they are taught by certain teachers. Boles and Troen (2003) suggest that "egalitarianism is the pervasive myth that every teacher is as good as every other teacher" (p. 2). If the school as an organization is to provide quality education for all students, improvement will depend on quality instruction being consistently implemented across all classrooms (Sanders, 1998). Teacher leaders can work in collaboration with other teachers and influence them to make their practice public so that these inequities are evident and can be addressed.

Figure 2.2. Uneven Student Assessment Results

Course	Teacher	Percentage of Students Who Meet the Assessment Criteria
American Government	1	44%
American Government	2	100%
American Government	3	58%
American Government	4	57%
English I	1	90%
English I	2	59%
English I	3	100%
English I	4	81%
English I	5	81%
English I	6	11%

Improve Teacher Quality

Teacher leadership is a means to move teaching toward a higher level of professionalism. Leading and learning are closely aligned, so as teachers take on leadership roles, they learn, and as they learn, they lead. This is why it is important to consider how all teachers can assume leadership roles. Given the right circumstances, even teachers who are not as skilled as others may not only provide leadership but also improve their own instructional skills. The adage of "we learn what we teach" holds true for everyone.

Reduce Attrition of Teachers

From the Field In my school, the accomplished administrators serve as magnets for NBCTs to come to our high-needs school. We are given support and freedom to use our expertise to help our students succeed. How can we replicate this professional situation in other high-needs schools?

Joan Celestino, NBCT
Eighth Grade Language Arts Teacher
Winston-Salem, North Carolina

No school can afford the attrition of talented faculty, because it is becoming more difficult to find quality teachers. However, Ingersoll and Smith (2003) estimated in their study of teacher turnover that 40 to 50 percent of beginning teachers leave education within five years. Over 78 percent of these teachers cite four areas of inadequate working conditions: student discipline problems, lack of support from school administration, poor student motivation, and lack of teacher influence over schoolwide and classroom decision making (p. 13). Each of these working conditions reflects the absence of a collaborative school culture. Teachers stay in schools where they feel a sense of belonging and are offered opportunities to be contributing members to the organization. There is a positive relationship between teacher leadership and teacher commitment and retention (Pounder et al., 1995, cited in York-Barr & Duke, 2004). A higher level of commitment from teachers results when teachers are involved in authentic professional participation.

Benefit from Diverse Leadership Styles

Principals who deal with teachers unwilling to change often say, "If only that teacher would retire." Many of these teachers are not incompetent, but they have average or mediocre skills. Principals cannot simply wait around for them to retire. It is better to put energy into encouraging them to become good teachers. Here is where diverse leadership styles and social networks can make a difference. Just like students responding to different types of teaching styles, teachers are influenced by different leadership styles. In many cases, a teacher leader may influence another teacher whom the principal is unable to reach for whatever reason. Providing a variety of leadership styles will increase the likelihood that teachers will improve their practice.

The School

Reduce the Power Struggles

When the goals of the principal and the teachers are not aligned, these "differences of opinion" can result in a power struggle. Symptoms of these conflicts may include withdrawal from interactions, conversations that are one-sided, or strong disagreements in public spaces. These relationships are not healthy for the school climate, and they can certainly make the principal feel uncomfortable.

Building teacher leadership will reduce power struggles in three ways. First, teachers will have more information on which to base decisions and will understand why decisions are made. Second, teacher leaders are usually those teachers who can communicate collective decisions effectively with others both within and outside the school. Finally, teachers who take on leadership roles and are more informed can move away from their dependence on the principal and assume responsibility for collective decisions rather than blaming unpopular ideas on the principal, central office, or other external policymakers.

Keep the Focus on the Improvement of Teaching and Learning

Teachers' work lives are busy and focused on their students' learning, so the most logical areas in which teachers might be willing to lead are related to instruction. This helps address the principal's dilemma of balancing both management and instructional leadership responsibilities. With the current emphasis on improved achievement for all students, principals cannot ignore instructional leadership tasks; however, they do not have to be alone in leading all the work related to improved student learning when teachers can keep the focus on this goal. Teacher leaders can be significant sources of advocacy and support for instructional practices intended to improve student learning. Without teacher advocacy, the work of convincing already overloaded teachers that they should invest time and energy in developing new classroom practices will be more difficult, if not impossible.

Use Limited Resources Effectively

Most of us would agree that there is more work to do in a school than there are people to do it. With reduced resources and few discretionary funds, the principal must create novel ways to increase services to students. The most overlooked and underused resource in most schools is the professional staff. Creating a context in which teachers increase their capacity as skilled leaders will result in a commensurate increase in resources, such as more effective use of materials and equipment and careful selection of programs that align with organizational goals.

Accomplish the Accountability Agenda

The "Accountability Agenda" is often translated into "increased student test scores." Although the quality of current measures of this success—standardized tests—is debatable, few of us would argue against the need for accountability. In spite of the focus on testing, most accountability systems at the state level, and even more so at the local level, involve more than test scores. Accountability measures and other assessment instruments can provide data to aid in decision making regarding what instructional practices, organizational patterns, curricular emphases, and/or instructional materials best improve performance. A principal can facilitate this process of using data for decision making, but teacher leaders will contribute significantly in attaching meaning to the data and turning that meaning into classroom actions.

Sustain Continuous Improvement

Most school systems fail to recognize the importance of leadership stability and leadership succession. Repeatedly, studies have demonstrated that a strong instructional leader can influence schools to increase their effectiveness (Cotton, 2003), but longitudinal studies have also demonstrated that when these strong instructional leaders exit the school, the improvement agenda is slowed or halted, and in some cases even reversed (Hargreaves & Fink, 2004). When efforts have been made to develop teacher leaders, the school's improvement program has a much greater chance of surviving changes in formal leadership. As teacher leadership grows within a school, the organization can become more self-monitoring and self-improving. In fact, teacher leaders often induct and inform new principals about the work of their organization so that the support of improved teaching and learning continues (Goodbread, 2000).

The Principal's Role

Help Address the Principal's Ever-Expanding Job

Principals who succeed know they did not accomplish that success singlehandedly, because schools are too complex for one or even a few people to lead. Anyone who has been a principal for more than a year knows that each year brings more responsibilities. It is highly unlikely that help will come in the form of additional administrative positions; rather, it is more probable that the principal will be asked to make better use of the limited human resources already in place. The "superprincipal myth" (Copland, 2001, p. 528) must give way to engaging all teachers in varying levels of leadership so that principals can survive. If principals are to meet these ever-expanding demands, they need help. Teachers who assume various leadership roles are significant players in helping the principal succeed—or not. Whether teacher leadership is focused on individual classroom instructional responsibilities or schoolwide issues, it helps assure the success of the whole system, including the principal.

Distinguish Principals as Leaders of Leaders

When teachers expand their leadership influence as they engage in school system projects, external networks within large-scale programs, and professional organizations, they become emissaries for the school. In turn, principals are viewed by the external leaders of these initiatives as innovative because of their work to improve schools with the help of excellent teacher leaders. In time, these teachers may be chosen to take on larger leadership roles in another school or at the school system level. As difficult as it is to lose talented teacher leaders, principals have more to gain by encouraging teachers to move into these more challenging roles than to discourage them, even if it means the loss of their skills and abilities. These are the conditions that cause principals to be perceived as leaders of leaders.

Summary

Teacher leadership is ubiquitous and can be overlooked by principals and other formal leaders within both the school and the school system. In spite of this, the proliferation of teacher leader roles demonstrates how these teachers are gradually being recognized as an untapped resource for improved teaching and learning. In the vignette about Markham Middle School, we saw how both informal and formal teacher leadership can emerge if there is support. Investing energy, time, and resources into this new way of leading and learning can result in numerous benefits for individual teachers, the school as a whole, and the principal.

This is not easy work. It demands a commitment from the principal to make it happen. Knowing what the roadblocks to building a culture of change are along the way will help make the journey easier. In the next chapter, we invite principals to consider predictable phases of the change, individual reactions to change, and how to prepare relevant others.

Resources

2.1 Teacher Leaders Network—This network provides access to teacher leadership resources as well as an electronic mailing list for accomplished teacher leaders. Retrieved on September 25, 2005, from http://www.teacherleaders.org

2.2 Tapped In—Website that provides online professional learning tools, resources, connections to colleagues, and support. Retrieved on September 25, 2005, from http://tappedin.org/tappedin/

2.3 Teacher Leadership Project—Network to help teacher leaders integrate technology into the curriculum. Retrieved on September 25, 2005, from http://www.esd189.org/tlp/

2.4 Teachers Network Leadership Institute—Network of teacher leaders who advocate for education. Retrieved on September 25, 2005, from http://www.teachersnetwork.org/tnpi/

2.5 Center for Teacher Leadership: Organizations—Provides access information for key teacher leadership organizations. Retrieved on September 26, 2005, from http://www.ctl.vcu.edu/organizations.htm

2.6 About ED: Educational Association and Organizations—The U.S. Department of Education provides contact information for professional associations and organizations. Retrieved on September 25, 2005, from http:/www.ed.gov/about/contacts/gen/othersites/associations.html

2.7 Center for Teaching Quality—Provides support for teacher quality and teacher leadership. Retrieved on September 25, 2005, from http://www.teachingquality.org/

3

Developing a Culture of Continuous Improvement

Schools cannot maintain the status quo for many reasons. Demands from the larger system and, more important, from changing student needs require continuous improvement and ongoing changes. Principals can feel overwhelmed leading uncontrollable changes. On top of this, school staff members determine programmatic or operational changes that are controllable but equally challenging to put into place. Promoting teacher leadership introduces a deliberate, local change in the power structure that engages teachers as partners in collective decisions addressing difficult problems facing schools. Instructing student populations whose demographics are rapidly changing, bringing special needs students into the learning mainstream, and ensuring that all students are taught by quality teachers generate issues on a day-to-day basis. Only professional staff members who live with these problems can design solutions and put them into practice. The goal of the work advocated in this book is to build a system through which collective effort continues and change is sustained, even after the principal leaves.

See
Resource 3.1
Page 59.

To prepare for this type of leadership, it is wise to understand the complexity of building a culture of change. In this chapter, we will first examine the phases through which individuals move when they confront a new way of working. Next, we look at how individuals' differences can influence their passages through the phases of change. Then we address other entities principals need to get ready for this change, such as the administrative team and the central office leader. Finally, we offer advice to principals about staying on target with the long-term commitment necessary to fully realize this new view of leadership.

We believe that principals can take intentional actions to build teacher leadership; however, there are predictable risks involved in moving from being the person who is responsible for all the answers to facilitating many problem solvers—teacher leaders. Disrupting the current way of doing work makes people anxious. Asking teachers to take ownership of problems upsets their expectations of what a principal is supposed to do, and there will be predictable reactions to these changes. There will most likely be teacher actions to undermine a change in leadership methods. If principals are aware of these possible reactions, they can be prepared rather than being blindsided.

If the purpose of making change is to improve student learning, then change will be continuous, based on the diverse needs of students and teachers. Not only are principals introducing a new way of leading, but they are most probably also endorsing a new way of professional learning. As teachers learn and take on leadership roles, they will feel discomfort because they will be asked to examine their beliefs, attitudes, knowledge, and skills in order to improve student learning. Effective principals balance an understanding of teachers' disequilibrium with continuing to press for change. Norton (2004) suggests that "this balancing act—this ability to set high expectations while building a professional relationships with teachers—is the hallmark of today's successful principal" (p. 2). These are complex changes, and it is not easy work.

We believe that principals can be skillful in leading planned change. The first step is to study the schools' history of change management and how this history influences teachers' willingness to be involved in another project. We then provide an overview of what is known about how teachers generally react to change, depending on factors that influence an individual's reaction to change such as their adult development, career situation, philosophy of teaching and learning, and personal issues. Everyone resists change, but people respond differently to change initiatives depending on their personal circumstances. We provide several interventions principals may use depending on the context and teachers' individual needs.

A History of Change

See
Tool 3.1
Page 60.

A major contributing factor to whether or not a change will be successful in a school is the school's history of change efforts (Fullan, 2003). Not surprisingly, where there is a history of success, new proposals have a greater chance of succeeding. If previous change initiatives have fared poorly, new proposals are likely to suffer the same fate. Teachers' lack of enthusiasm may be influenced by past experiences with contrived involvement, so they protect themselves to prevent being disappointed again.

Even the most eager teachers will be hesitant if there is a history of multiple innovations that subsequently lack the support to put them into full implementation. A history of failed changes does not mean it will be impossible to initiate change, but principals should be cautious regarding the pace and what assistance needs to be in place. If a school has multiple change initiatives under way, each should be clearly identified. This may reveal that there have been fragmented efforts and that consolidating or even discarding particular initiatives is needed. Teacher leadership and learning are not programs, but form the foundation for how program initiatives are introduced, supported, and continued. There must be an integration of this new way of leading and learning with the existing initiatives.

Themes Common to the Change Process

We identify four common themes based on three widely referenced models of the change process: Bridges' (1991) recommendations for managing transitions, rather than managing change; Fullan's (2003) advice for initiating, implementing, and continuing an initiative; and the work of Hall and Hord (2001) in supporting teachers as they move through "Stages of Concern." Even with their unique perspectives, each model supports the following themes related to change which can be used to guide principals in their work with teachers.

> **From the Field** Any time that I am trying to create change in instruction and teacher growth, I try to realize that teachers are like students. They all learn at different rates, in different ways, and at different times.
>
> *Michelle Pedogo*
> Middle School Principal
> MiddleWeb Diary

- *Change is a personal phenomenon.* Most principals know that they cannot announce changes and then expect everyone to fully adopt them. Instead "change is a process through which people and organizations move as they gradually come to understand and become skilled and competent in the use of the new ways" (Hall & Hord,

2001, p. 5). It is the individual teacher that changes, not the school. For this reason, principals can strategically plan for individual needs in order to achieve organizational change. Attempts to bring about change in schools that ignore the individual result in resistance and wasted resources.

- *There are discernable stages.* The change process does not happen immediately; instead, there are distinct phases. For example, Bridges (1991) points out, letting go of beliefs and behaviors is necessary before new ways of working can occur. Even principals seeking to successfully implement a new view of leadership must be ready to let go of old ways of working and move toward new behaviors themselves in order to facilitate this process for others.

- *Time is a factor.* Fullan (2003) found that in schools "even moderately complex changes take from 3 to 5 years" (p. 52). The time needed for change increases from elementary school to middle school and high school levels. Too often, leaders abandon initiatives when they do not see immediate results. There must be a trust in the process to encourage teachers to believe that the change is not a passing fad.

- *Intentional actions can move the process in the desired direction.* The leader's actions or interventions can keep the change process going; more specifically, the selection of particular actions will guide the speed, direction, and acceptance of the changes. This reinforces the notion that teacher leading and learning are successful when principals are intentional in their own leadership.

Three Predictable Stages

Considering these themes, principals can be prepared to help teachers move through three stages of change: getting started, trying it out, and accepting a new way of doing business. We provide selected actions that principals can use in promoting, building, and sustaining teacher leading and learning.

Stage 1: Getting Started

- *Start with the problem, rather than the change.* Teachers will respond to problems that they see as important to them before they will accept a change or solution that appears to have no link to their work. Looking at problems or needs may result in conversations about how the school faculty and staff could work together differently to address them.

- *Determine which individuals will lose something.* Identifying who has a vested interest in the current system will help principals be aware of sources of resistance regarding the change.

- *Recognize that everyone will lose something.* People will feel loss. Even the changes we want require that we let go of or leave behind current ways.

- *Be prepared for anger, anxiety, and other emotions.* Too often, principals approach teachers with logical explanations about why there is a need for change or try to talk teachers out of their feelings. People experiencing loss do not hear the logic, but instead need emotional support. Listening is a more powerful tool than explaining.

- *Provide differentiated support.* If change depends on individual teachers, then the support must be geared to the teachers who have the highest levels of concern. Providing reassurance is crucial for these teachers.

- *Be positive at all times about the change.* Teachers can discern how sincere the principal is about advocating a change initiative. A negative comment or uncertainty will be picked up quickly as a cue that perhaps things will go back to the way they were.

- *Honor the past, but show a future connected to students.* Acknowledging that the past was not bad, just unresponsive to the needs of current students, helps teachers who are feeling remorse as the principal encourages a new way of leading and learning. Finding ways to celebrate and let go of the past moves teachers toward a new way of working.

Stage 2: Trying It Out

- *Provide tangible examples.* Invite teachers into conversations about how teacher leading and learning will look. Send a team of teachers to visit similar schools where the principals and teachers collectively work together. These concrete examples can spark conversations upon their return.

- *Build supportive structures.* Schools are busy places, and unless there are structures in place to support teacher leadership, such as routine and dependable committees, teams, and task groups, change will not happen. No one can change another person, but principals can facilitate the building of relationships through structures that bring teachers together.

- *Communicate again and again.* Teachers know the principal is serious about change if there is consistency in communication. For example, when speaking with teachers, parents, students, and others, the principal can remind everyone how teacher leadership is an underused resource that will no longer be ignored.

■ *Exert both pressure and support.* During this stage, many teachers will want to abandon this new way of working together because there will be conflicts, time constraints, and uncertainty. The principal's leadership is most needed at this point, because it may take gentle pressure and support to keep moving forward.

■ *Try to limit additional changes.* Sometimes a principal cannot avoid asking teachers to take on more change because of external demands. However, there should be an effort to limit the number of changes teachers experience as they start to lead and learn together. If externally initiated changes intrude, it may be necessary to put local initiatives on hold or at a maintenance level.

■ *Learn leadership skills together.* As colearners, principals and teachers can acquire the requisite leadership skills needed to work together. With the current emphasis on collaborative work in schools, there are numerous resources that principals can tap into for leadership development.

■ *Celebrate successes and mistakes.* Most people like to celebrate successes, but growth in leadership depends on learning from mistakes. To show disappointment when a teacher makes a wrong decision will send messages to all teachers that taking a risk as a leader is dangerous. Instead, principals can show how these mistakes are valuable lessons in building leadership.

Stage 3: Accepting a New Way of Doing Business

■ *Frequently remind everyone about the purpose for a new way of leading and learning.* Teacher leadership will be expanded in this stage. The communication necessary within the previous stage is just as critical, because new people will be engaged.

■ *Compare Stage 1 with Stage 3.* If teachers can see concrete examples of how the faculty has increased in their leading and learning, they can better appreciate their efforts. This assures teachers that this way of working will not go away.

■ *Provide recognition.* We are continuously amazed at how often teacher leaders report the lack of recognition in their schools. Principals can find ways to recognize teachers' leading and learning either publicly or privately, depending on the teachers and the school culture.

- *Continue support.* Principals will relinquish part of the responsibility for promoting and building teacher leadership as teachers take on more of this responsibility. However, there is still a need for ongoing support from the formal leader, such as making adjustments to structures and the use of resources.

- *Plan to sustain the change.* Helping teacher leaders to plan for transitions can make a difference for the school and the school system. Involving teachers in a conversation on how to sustain change as formal leadership changes may result in continuing support of teacher leadership. Teacher leaders, regardless of their competence and years of experience, are hesitant in their leadership when a new principal arrives.

Deliberate leadership actions in each of these stages can help to achieve valued outcomes. Remember, outcomes valued by some people are not necessarily valued by everyone—consequently, different reactions to change are inevitable. Some teachers will quickly embrace this new view of leadership, others will be cautious, and a few may reject the idea altogether.

Individual Reactions

When any change is introduced, some teachers may be so enthused that they volunteer to lead study groups or visit other schools, while other teachers go to great lengths to avoid any professional conversations about the change initiatives. As previously discussed, we can predict that most everyone will move through stages of change, but they certainly do not all move at the same rate. It may be difficult to match specific support for each individual teacher's needs, but examining reasons for these differences can help principals to accept, or at least tolerate, the diversity of perspectives and plan for levels of support for the majority of teachers.

We recommend that principals consider why teachers may or may not be motivated to lead. There are four areas in which teachers' differences can influence their willingness to lead and learn. The first area we examine is the teachers' adult growth and development through systems that explain their "ways of knowing" (Drago-Severson, 2004, p. 24) that influence how they will react to change. We suggest strategies to support teachers within each system during a change process. Next we consider where the teachers are in their career cycles (Steffy, Wolfe, Pasch, & Enz, 1999). Then we identify some of the myriad personal issues that compete for teachers' attention. Finally, we recommend that principals acknowledge and accept that teachers do not always share the same philosophy of teaching and learning.

Adult Growth and Development

Drago-Severson (2004) studied 25 principals who supported teacher professional learning and used Kegan's (1994) constructive-developmental theory to understand how the principals' work supported teacher growth and development. Using this model, principals can better understand how teachers "construct—*or actively make sense of*—the reality in which they live (with respect to cognitive, interpersonal, and intrapersonal development)" (p. 24).

From the Field I could not have done it without an administrator who understood how adults learn and was willing to take a chance in helping me implement this professional development plan.

Carolann Wade, NBCT
TLN Member
Raleigh, North Carolina

These categories, while not rigid, offer descriptions of behaviors that will help principals recognize how teachers differ in constructing their realities. This allows principals to take advantage of the strengths teachers bring to the process.

Previously, we referred to "time" as one of the themes of change. In addition to examining teachers' adult growth and development, it is important to consider how much time it may take for them to adopt change. Several authors have developed descriptions of different types of people and the amount of time that it takes them to move through a change process; we believe that the "labels" (Figure 3.1) selected by these authors help to visualize and identify behaviors. In this section, we focus on Schlechty's (1993) types and intervention strategies adapted from his work.

Figure 3.1. Time It Takes People to Adopt a Change

Source	*Little Time*				*A Lot of Time*
Rogers (2003)	Innovators	Early adopters	Early majority	Late majority	Laggards
Quaglia (1991)	Yahoos		Yes/Buts		Come-ons
Schlechty (1993)	Trail-blazers	Pioneers	Settlers	Stay-at-homes	Saboteurs
Whitaker (2002)	Superstars		Backbones		Mediocres
Joyce, Mueller, Hrycauk, & Hrycauk (2005)	Gourmet omnivores	Active consumers	Passive consumers		Reticent consumers

Instrumental Way of Knowing (Drago-Severson, 2004).

These adults are primarily oriented toward their own self-interests, purposes, and wants. They are less likely to see the perspectives of other people unless those perspectives interfere with what they want themselves. They will adopt change only if they see it is in their best interests. The teachers who view the world through this lens might be called "stay-at-homes" (Schlechty, 1993). These are the teachers who do not easily give up what they are doing for something new. Principals will notice that these teachers are cynical and cautious, and use their energy to resist the change rather than adopt it. Their skepticism can be viewed as strength when these teachers' critical questions require principals and others to provide a rationale for change. Strategies principals can use with these teachers include the following:

- At first, limit the time and energy spent with resistant teachers while always extending the invitation to be a part of the effort.
- Invite peers who have adopted the change and are valued by these teachers to work with them.
- Provide as much information as the teachers need so that they will believe that the change is safe to adopt. (Adapted from Schlechty, 1993, pp. 49–50)

Socializing Way of Knowing (Drago-Severson, 2004).

This system may represent the majority of teachers in most schools. These teachers depend on external authority and seek approval from the principal or peers who influence them. In addition, these teachers are sensitive to their own feelings and the feelings of others. They derive satisfaction from their involvement with other teachers. These "settlers" (Schlechty, 1993) are not going to be out in front when change is taking place. Their strength is their ability to ask for realistic examples of the change. Strategies principals might consider in working with these teachers include the following:

- Help the teachers know what the expectations are for them.
- Develop support systems that prevent them from quitting when the work becomes frustrating.
- Design recognition strategies that can be used to celebrate achieved benchmarks in the change. (Adapted from Schlechty, 1993, p. 49)

Self-Authoring Way of Knowing (Drago-Severson, 2004).

These teachers evaluate and criticize themselves based on internally generated values and standards. Rather than seeking the approval of others, they are concerned with their own competence and performance and see conflict as potentially useful in clarifying issues. These teachers may separate into two groups of change agents. The first group includes those who are "trailblazers" (Schlechty, 1993). These are the teachers who love risk and are motivated by new ideas. They do not need to know what is expected of them; in fact, they take off without a plan. However, they still need a connection to the formal leadership, especially the principal. These teachers may isolate themselves from the rest of the teachers and be viewed as preoccupied with their own agendas. Strategies principals can use to support these teachers include the following:

- Find unique ways to provide support, such as connecting them with external networks of like-minded teachers.

- Encourage them to see their work in the context of the mission of the school, rather than isolated from other teachers.

- Capture what these teachers are doing to help other teachers when they adopt the change. (Adapted from Schlechty, 1993, pp. 47–48)

The second group of teachers in this system might be called "pioneers" (Schlechty, 1993). These teachers are often motivated by the "trailblazers" and are willing to take risks, but with a little more caution. In this group are the teacher leaders who are respected by their peers and who can influence others to move in the direction of the change. When they adopt a change, there is a good chance that others who have not yet done so will join or seriously consider it. Strategies principals can use to support these teachers include the following:

- Provide encouragement that adopting the change will make a difference in student learning.

- Invite them to see demonstration lessons.

- Offer resources so that they can build collaborative groups. (Adapted from Schlechty, 1993, pp. 48–49)

See
Resource 3.2
Page 59.

The final group of teachers exhibit the strongest resistance toward change. It is difficult to link their behaviors to a system or "way of knowing" because these teachers take on these roles for a variety of reasons that may not relate to where they are in their adult growth and development. The best term we found in the literature for these teachers is "saboteurs" (Schlechty, 1993, p. 50), because they undermine and attempt to destroy change efforts they believe should not take place. Often they have been repeatedly disappointed with so many change initiatives that they refuse to be involved in the process and try to influence other teachers not be involved either. Practical strategies for principals to consider when dealing with this type of resistor include the following:

- Listen to find out the cause of their resistance.
- Do not ignore them; attempt to bring them into the conversations about the change even if they are disagreeable.
- Do not reward them by not asking them to take on responsibilities expected of other teachers. (Adapted from Schlechty, 1993, p. 5)

See Resource 3.3 Page 49.

Using what is known about adult development and its impact on how teachers accept or resist change can help principals to feel less frustrated when they are faced with an unwillingness to change. It does not make it any easier, but at least principals will understand teachers' needs regarding pressure, resources, and encouragement. The good news is that "people (and their constructions of reality) can *change or develop* over time with developmentally appropriate supports and challenges" (Drago-Severson, 2004, p. 24). In order to develop strategies to nurture and confront teachers' unwillingness to continuously improve, principals and teacher leaders must be knowledgeable about adult growth and development. Smith (2003) developed a matrix (Figure 3.2) to describe how this balancing of support and challenge must be purposeful. Too much of either support or challenge can be counterproductive.

From the Field There are the "movers and the shakers," who readily jump on board when asked to help out; the "fence sitters," who weigh the benefits as well as the time commitment, but sometimes can be nudged along to participate in a school-wide effort; and, then, there are the "nay-sayers," who, for whatever reasons, will just limit their involvement in school initiatives…. One of my most important responsibilities is to keep working on the "fence sitters" to become new "movers and shakers"….

Carol Stack
Middle School Principal
MiddleWeb Diary

Figure 3.2. Balance Between Support and Challenge

High challenge and low support	Sufficient challenge and support
Stress Feels very critical; disempowers the individual Feels competitive	Motivational, learning, developmental
Low challenge and low support	**Too much support and low challenge**
Boring, distant, absent, avoidant	Stifling, patronizing, controlling

Key Skills for Coaching, by J. V. Smith, 2003, p. 4. Copyright 2003 by Anaptys Ltd. Used with permission.

Where teachers are in their adult growth and development is only one piece of the puzzle in understanding teacher differences. There are other aspects of teachers' lives that influence their willingness to lead and learn. Next we will examine where teachers are in their career and how this may influence them.

Teaching Career

Principals cannot make assumptions about who will be willing to lead. Many beginning teachers these days are mature adults who decide to move from a previous profession to teaching. Consequently, there may be teachers who are "self-authoring" in their adult growth and development but entering the classroom for the first time as a teacher. One might predict that those teachers who are just beginning to teach may be somewhat reluctant to take on new roles beyond their survival in the classroom. Yet there are first-year teachers who reach out for leadership roles in order to end their isolation and feel a part of a collaborative community. Some teachers nearing retirement may lack interest in starting something new; others may take on responsibilities because they want to leave a professional legacy. In between these two extremes in a teacher's career are different phases along a continuum toward increasing competence. Teacher leaders can emerge from every phase of the career cycle.

As expected, teachers do not move through all career phases, but acknowledging the needs of teachers at different places along the continuum can help principals understand why individuals at different points in their career might need different types of activities to address their concerns or support their growth to a higher level of competence. Based on the work of Steffy, Wolfe, Pasch, and Enz (1999), we provide brief descriptions of teachers' career phases as well as strategies that may be helpful in the support of teacher leaders.

Apprentice Teacher

Apprentice teachers are in their first three years of teaching. They are gaining skills and confidence, but they still experience much self-doubt. They often volunteer for activities outside the classroom and are usually open to new ideas. They may be ready to accept leadership responsibilities this early in their career, depending on their adult growth and development. Mentor assignments may facilitate the involvement of beginning teachers in activities that will prepare them for future leadership.

Professional Teacher

Professional teachers are competent, solid, and dependable. They form the majority of the faculty in most schools, and few have aspirations for administrative positions. They view their greatest reward as student feedback, specifically through individual notes, visits, and calls from former students. They see their peers as colleagues. Many teachers in this career phase are ready for leadership roles that will provide the additional challenge they need to avoid boredom in their jobs.

Expert Teacher

Expert teachers move beyond competence to a level of instinctively knowing what to do with students from all backgrounds and with a variety of needs. Many of these teachers seek and achieve national certification; all of them demonstrate the knowledge and skills for this certification. They look for new ideas to improve teaching and learning and become involved in the profession beyond the school at the local, state, and national levels. Principals will not have to encourage these teachers to be leaders because, through their own initiative, they are leaders. Expert teachers need the resources to allow them to expand their leadership. Many teachers in this career phase are concerned about leaving a legacy and are anxious to mentor less experienced teachers.

Distinguished Teacher

Distinguished teachers influence policy and legislation at the local, state, and national levels. They are individuals who are consulted by decision makers. They are often award winners in teaching. Teachers in this phase have moved beyond the school level in their leadership, so they should be encouraged to continue this work. Action research is an avenue through which distinguished teachers can influence practice and satisfy their interest in moving beyond the traditional forms of professional development.

At any phase, teachers may move into stages of withdrawal. Being able to diagnose the level of withdrawal can help principals to select appropriate interventions so that the withdrawal might be prevented or at least decreased in intensity. Steffy and colleagues (1999) identify three levels of withdrawal: initial, persistent, and deep.

Initial

Teaching is adequate, but the teacher begins to experience feelings of inadequacy and decreased competence. The teacher becomes quieter and more isolated even during group gatherings. Individuals may not be aware of what is happening to them.

Persistent

At this stage, the withdrawal moves to active criticism and even obstructionist behaviors. These teachers often demonstrate strong resistance to change and sometimes serve as gatekeepers, keeping out any changes to which they wish to be unresponsive or resistant.

Deep

In deep withdrawal, teachers spiral downward in their attitudes and skills. Professional growth is no longer a part of their development and they often become "defensive and difficult." (Adapted from Steffy et al., 1999, pp. 15–17)

Understanding these phases of withdrawal offers principals an explanation for behaviors that before may have caused them exasperation and anger. As soon as a principal identifies a teacher in initial withdrawal, steps should be taken to bring the teacher back to his or her level of competence. In the busy lives of principals, it is easy to overlook these early symptoms and to rely on teachers to "fix themselves," but in many cases relatively simple actions by the principal can re-engage the teacher. These actions may include the following:

- Inviting the teacher to participate in an off-site professional learning event.
- Engaging the teacher in a task force focused on an issue of concern to the teacher.
- Stopping by the teacher's classroom frequently to have conversations about issues unrelated to their teaching.
- Putting in the teacher's mailbox interesting articles related to an interest of the teacher.

Other influences on a teacher's willingness to lead come from outside the school. Individuals at different points in their personal life experience stresses and conditions that may cause them to react differently.

Personal Issues

Teachers may want to commit to leading, but other parts of their lives can cause them to be reluctant, or perhaps even resist or withdraw. These pressures come from external sources and from intrapersonal stress the teacher is experiencing. Regardless of the source, balancing personal and professional lives is tough, especially for leaders.

External Demands

Teachers' lives extend beyond the school building walls and are influenced by demands in their personal lives. Pressures that require attention come from family, community, and other commitments. Presently, the teaching population is heavily distributed at the beginning of and at the end of the teaching career. Both ends of the continuum have personal concerns that distract from work situations. Younger teachers may have childcare issues that rule out early morning or late afternoon meetings; whereas older teachers may be responsible for elder care.

These family demands usually take priority; many teachers are reluctant to let added school responsibilities take precedence over such issues. Some teachers may face situations in which they are discouraged by family members from taking on additional leadership roles or even working outside the home (Zinn, 1997). Volunteering in community organizations often provides greater satisfaction for teachers than taking on additional work responsibilities. Finally, there are issues with personal health or the health of family members that drain teachers' emotional and physical strength so that they are unable to offer their leadership.

Intrapersonal Demands

Not every teacher believes that they can be a leader. In school cultures, teachers are, in most cases, not encouraged to lead, especially by their peers. To lead may be viewed as being the "boss," and this would not help these teachers maintain relationships with their colleagues.

Philosophy of Teaching and Learning

See
Resources 3.4,
3.5
Page 60.

Many conflicts within schools can be traced to differences in beliefs about how students learn and what teaching strategies should be used. For example, when a new instructional strategy is introduced that requires teachers to follow a script, and the majority of teachers believe that students should learn through problem solving, there is resistance. Although most teachers study different philosophical traditions in their undergraduate programs, they seldom connect these to their disagreements with team members about how to address student needs. Until principals and teacher leaders bring these differences to the table for discussion, there may be passive or even aggressive resistance to changes in instruction.

Preparing Others

A change in the way of leading and learning should not be a surprise to other formal school leaders such as assistant principals, guidance directors, and others. Although primarily a school-based initiative, a number of external entities and groups will be affected by this change as well. Individual schools are part of larger systems, and a change in one part of the system affects the entire system. With a move toward distributed power and authority, others outside the school will need to be prepared for implementation of this new view of leadership. Proactively providing information and building relationships along the way are smart strategies for most any change initiative, large or small.

Principals are responsible for taking the steps necessary to create a state of readiness on the part of these entities. If done well, hardly anyone will notice; if done poorly, incompletely, or in a neglectful way, the negative results may never be overcome. We identify one internal group (the administrative team) and three external groups (the central office, parents and the community, and teachers' organizations) that principals need to prepare as the school's shared vision for leadership moves toward reality.

Administrative Teams

Administrative teams vary in definition from school to school. In some schools, the administrative team includes only the principal and assistant principals. In other schools, the team also includes lead teachers, guidance counselors, and other formal leaders. It is essential to provide clarity early on regarding the definition of teacher leaders in terms of who they are, what their responsibilities and authority will include, and how their work aligns with and is not in conflict with the administrative team. To have internal strife is to assure failure, even if external entities are supportive.

Principals, especially in larger schools, delegate formal leadership responsibilities to others, such as assistant principals, and these individuals often have the most frequent contact with classroom teachers. When principals are off-site, the assistant principals are the people who step in to support teacher leaders. Even though principals may sincerely believe in teacher

leadership, if other formal leaders are not in agreement with these beliefs, there will be problems. If they are to work to promote teacher leadership, the administrative team should be involved in substantive decision making.

See
Tool 3.2
Page 60.

If a principal is new to a school, an administrative team may already be in place; alternately, principals may have input into the selection of formal leaders. Regardless of the situation, it is the principal's responsibility to build relationships with the team to establish a unified support system for teacher leaders.

The Central Office

Keeping immediate supervisors informed regarding initiatives at the school site is always a wise idea. Watching the supervisors' reactions gives clues about the pace at which the principal should initiate change. While the new view of leadership is still at the "thinking stage," a meeting with the principal's immediate supervisor to get input and advice should be scheduled. Even if the conversation does not seem to produce much interest or enthusiasm from the supervisor, the principal has performed an important service in terms of building relationships with the central office and preparing them for the changes ahead. As the distribution of power and authority increases, teacher leaders will become primary contacts for various central office administrators. Making these officials aware of the change from one leader to many leaders will better prepare everyone.

The responsibility of the central office leaders is to keep the system in equilibrium. When a principal introduces changes that upset this balance, central office leaders may be unwilling to support the principal. Most central office leaders will support innovation as long as it does not negatively affect the larger system and they are kept informed.

Parents and the Community

Parents and community leaders get involved in schools when they believe it to be in their best interests. Distributing power and authority should be seen by external entities as the positive endeavor that it is. Parents need to know if a teacher leader will be taking major responsibility for a project or program involving their children. This information can be provided through letters, the school's website, telephone calls, electronic mail, newspaper articles, and face-to-face meetings. Teacher leaders should be introduced to parents and community members as the primary contact for the specific school initiatives they are leading. Knowing who the leaders are and how to contact them will help prepare parents and community members to understand this new view of leadership.

Teachers' Organizations

Teachers' organizations are important entities to involve regarding the distribution of power and authority. It is important to make sure that everyone understands that additional layers of administration are not being created, that teachers are not being overloaded with additional responsibilities, and that the necessary work does not infringe on contracted workloads. These issues need to be shared, understood, and evaluated frequently. This will go a long way in building and maintaining positive relationships with the leaders of teachers' organizations. Conversations regarding how this new view of leadership will impact items in the negotiated agreement need to begin early and involve representatives from the teachers' organization, the central office, and the school. Involving teacher leaders from the school will facilitate these conversations. Teachers should not be put in a position of dividing their loyalties between their work at the building site and their membership in their professional association.

Making the Long-Term Commitment: Advice for Staying on Target

As we bring this chapter to a close, it is important to re-emphasize that the work to be undertaken must be intentionally led, but the way principals do this will depend on their tenure with the school and the school system. Principals are in a variety of situations as they begin this effort, and there is no one set of experiences or circumstances that is ideal for the journey. We have provided "Good News/Challenging News" in Figure 3.3 to describe various circumstances in which principals might find themselves. Each of the situations can be positive and in support of the work; simultaneously each of the situations presents challenges. We invite principals to find their own situations on the chart and use this information as they make decisions about their work with teacher leaders.

Figure 3.3. Good News/Challenging News

Principal's Situation	Good News	Challenging News
New principal in this school, but worked as a principal in another school in the same school system	Do not have to unlearn ways of leading; "style" is open to develop without restraint from the past experience in this school.	Need to devote a good percentage of time and energy getting to know the school.
Current principal in the school	Can focus on the change itself because much of the job is routine.	May make too many assumptions about a situation. In doing this, may overlook important opportunities.
Worked as a principal before, but new to the school system and school	Everyone is expecting new ideas of operating within the school system and the school.	There is much about the individuals and the organization both in the school and the school system that is not known. Well-intended but naïve actions could generate resistance.
New to the school with no previous experience as a principal	What an opportunity to redefine the leadership roles in the school! There is no "history." An excellent context for change.	There is much to learn and the year will be very busy focused on just surviving. There may be little time and energy for nurturing others.

The principles that provide the framework for the chapters that follow are not issues that result from hopes, wishes, and waiting to see. If positive relationships are to be developed, power and authority to be distributed, and teacher leadership to be aligned with professional learning, then planned change must be undertaken. There may be individual teachers who push too hard to make these planned outcomes realities; there may be others who work diligently to keep them from ever being realized. Then there will be the "mass in the middle"—open to, but cautious about, the planned changes. They will be expecting strong leadership to get started, and they will require supportive conditions as things get under way.

Here is advice for principals as they commit to the implementation of the changes required to usher in this new view of leadership:

- *Raise the difficult questions.* There will be times when information from external and internal sources will have to be shared that will not be welcomed, even by the principal. Principals can develop the "capacity to deliver disturbing news and raise difficult questions in a way that people can absorb, prodding them to take up the message rather than ignore it or kill the messenger" (Heifetz & Linsky, 2002, p. 12).

- *Be persistent.* The changes involved in successfully implementing this new view of leadership are complex and will take time, perhaps years. Not everyone will be excited about everything and not all things will go well. Others will be looking to the principal to see if this change is really important or just something that gets time and attention when nothing else is happening.

- *Be flexible in leadership style.* Principals need to be prepared to exercise a variety of leadership styles to successfully implement planned changes. Depending on what is happening and who is involved, principals should be prepared to function both as a directive leader and a facilitative leader, as well as sometimes using an artful mixture of both styles.

See
Resource 3.6
Page 60.

- *Stay focused.* With the "busyness" of schools, it will be easy to be distracted by any number of issues and be unable to keep conversations and work focused on the school's shared vision of leadership. But if the principal stays focused, teachers will stay focused. Principals can take actions that keep these planned changes at the top of the daily agenda and minimize the distractions.

- *Align decisions about resources.* Once the school members develop a shared vision for student learning, the principal's work is to make sure that resources are aligned with this ideal. Looking at the current situation compared with this ideal inevitably reveals discrepancies. The principal must secure resources and facilitate collective decision making that aligns these resources in ways that reduce the gap between the existing and the ideal student learning outcomes.

Summary

To continuously improve practices, the faculty and staff must be involved in change. One approach to promote continuous improvement is to involve teachers in leadership responsibilities. If principals are moving from traditional leadership to the new view of leadership we are advocating, there will be change. Seeing the need for a change and successfully making that change happen do not necessarily travel together. With knowledge about the phases of change and how teachers individually experience change, principals are better prepared to lead with the intent of increasing teacher leading and learning.

Principals may acknowledge that individuals react differently to change, but this cannot keep them from moving forward with what is best for the students. It takes courage to face negative reactions, but the principal's job is to be focused and not waver from the goal regardless of the displeasure, complaints, and even anger that may emerge.

Resources

3.1 Education Topics: School Culture/Climate—The Association for Supervision and Curriculum Development (ASCD) provides an overview of school culture and climate, pulling from ASCD publications and other resources. Retrieved on September 25, 2005 from http://www.ascd.org/portal/site/ascd/menuitem.56b9a2dd41f 0500cbfb3ffdb62108a0c

3.2 Whitaker, T. W. (2002). *Dealing with difficult teachers* (2nd ed.). Larchmont, NY: Eye on Education—Addresses something that all principals face in their schools to one degree or another: difficult teachers. Includes strategies for motivating, creating discomfort in, communicating with, and reducing the influence of difficult teachers.

3.3 Conner, M. L. (2005). *How adults learn: Ageless learner, 1997–2004.* —Conner introduces the most significant concepts and terms in adult learning. Included in the work are an overview of adult learning theory, books on adult learning, and links to other websites. Retrieved April 14, 2005, from http://agelesslearner.com/intros/adultlearning.html

3.4 Zinn, L. M. (2001). A resource for teacher leadership: Philosophy of education inventory (PEI). In M. Katzenmeyer and G. Moller, *Awakening the sleeping giant: Helping teachers develop as leaders* (2nd ed.), 139–166. Thousand Oaks, CA: Corwin Press—Zinn's PEI provides teachers with an instrument that measures how they believe students learn and their preference for teaching methods. The instrument can be purchased directly from the author at Lifelong Learning Options, phone: (303) 499-0864.

3.5 Ferrero, D. J. (2005). Pathways to reform: Start with values. *Educational Leadership, 62*(5), 8–15—This article is a good companion when teachers are examining their educational philosophies.

3.6 Goleman, D., Boyatzis, R., & McKee, A. (2002). *Primal leadership: Realizing the power of emotional intelligence.* Boston: Harvard Business School Press—The authors explain how a leader's emotional intelligence can impact the organization. Six leadership styles and how each style may be required depending on the situation are described.

Tools

Tool 3.1   Charting the School's History of Change Initiatives

(See the chart on the facing page.)

Figure 3.4. Charting the School's History of Change Initiatives

Purpose: To visually display the history of change initiatives.

Materials needed: Table in Figure 3.4 prepared on butcher paper (10 feet wide) or a series of charts. Markers for each small group.

Directions:

1. Small groups of teachers in a faculty meeting write down all the change initiatives introduced within the last two to three years. Examples of change initiatives include curriculum programs, instructional strategies, and assessment tools.

2. Each group shares one change initiative at a time while a recorder posts the contributions in Columns A and B on the wall chart until all groups have shared all the initiatives they wrote down. Request that the groups not share duplicate initiatives.

3. In the large group, complete Columns C, D, E, F, and G for each initiative listed.

4. When the chart is completed through column G, the group can engage in a discussion of the history of change.

5. After evaluating the responses on the chart, the group can consider whether or not each initiative should continue. If the initiative is dropped or kept, the group should determine who will be affected by the action (Column I).

A Year(s)	B Change Initiative	C In Progress	D Successful /Ongoing	E Never Fully Implemented	F Stalled	G Failure	H Drop? (Y/N)	I Who Will Be Affected?

Tool 3.2 *Working with the Administrative Staff*

- *Invite* an outside facilitator to organize a retreat when all the administrators come together to examine this issue. Plan for at least two days, preferably at a pleasant location where everyone can stay overnight. Get away from the school setting. These retreats should be an annual event planned when other responsibilities will not intrude. Be sure to build fun into the experience.

- *Schedule* weekly staff meetings. Although this strategy is common, it is rarely treated as important, and often the meetings are interrupted and shortened due to pressing school business. Work with the clerical staff to develop their skills to deal with issues that can be delayed until the meeting is over.

- *Purchase* a large dining table with comfortable chairs and put it in an area where the teachers and administrators can use it for lunch. Although the teachers have the option of eating in this location, make a commitment with the administrators that after everyone has completed their lunch duties, they are to meet for lunch at this table. The informal conversation that happens during this time is often more valuable than formal meetings. Mix up the schedules if there are several lunch periods so that everyone gets an opportunity to visit with everyone else.

- *Plan* social activities, such as fishing or attending cultural events, with these leaders. Principals may believe they are to keep a distance from personal interactions, but if the principal understands that the purpose of these activities is to build camaraderie, then the experiences can be fun and serve that purpose.

- *Meet* one on one with assistant principals. When the administrative staff know that you care about them as individuals and value their diversity, there can be mutual respect. Not all administrators will believe that teachers should be involved as leaders or that they have the potential to make positive changes. Even with such a situation, an agreement can be reached to encourage rather than thwart your efforts. In fairness, these beliefs may be a result of the negative interactions they have had with teachers in the past. Most assistant principals are designed to handle the school problems, and this forces them to see mostly the negative side of human nature.

- *Pretend* you are going to leave your position at the school tomorrow. Every assistant principal should be prepared to take over your responsibilities. In order to leave a legacy, provide each administrator with professional development, important information, and your attention so that they can continue the initiatives started at the school.

Part 2

Putting the
Principles into Action

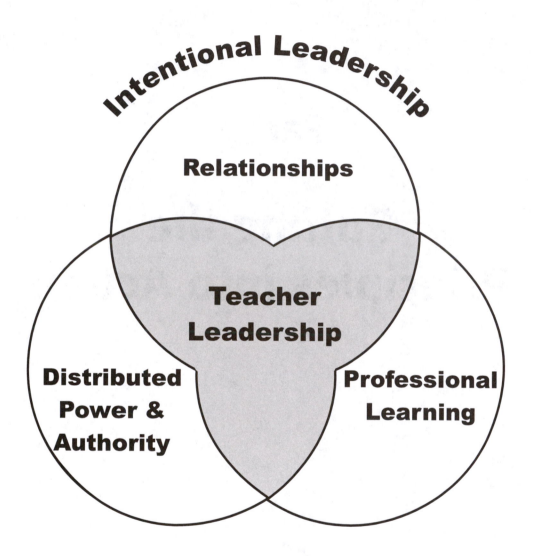

Part 2

Putting the
Principles into Action

In Part 2, the principles in the Framework for Intentional Leadership—building positive relationships, distributing power and authority, and aligning teacher leadership with professional learning—are addressed. Each chapter includes an introduction, self-study activities, and actions principals can take. Although these chapters may be read in any sequence, we recommend they be read in the order presented. We believe principals first pay attention to relationships before establishing structures for distributing power and authority. The foundation is then laid for the alignment of teacher leadership with professional learning.

Chapter 4, "Building Relationships," starts by asking principals to seek out existing human and social resources that can be used to increase teacher leading and learning. Attention is then given to how relationships can be built among teachers and between principals and teachers. Finally, there are suggestions on how to deal with the inevitable conflict that emerges as people collaborate. In Chapter 5, "Distributing Power and Authority," we ask principals to examine their beliefs and values about "letting go" of control. If principals acknowledge a desire to distribute power and authority, we offer strategies for working with teachers to develop a shared vision for student learning, collectively make decisions, and delegate effectively. We also recommend structures that principals can establish to facilitate the distribution of power and authority. Chapter 6, "Aligning Teacher Leadership and Professional Learning," invites principals to think differently about professional learning. Specific recommendations are provided for engaging teachers in leading and learning. At the end of this chapter, we address the reluctant teacher learners, those individuals who can no longer ignore their professional learning.

4

Building
Positive Relationships

Personal, professional, and social relationships support a web of school leadership. This web must be built on trust, or it is certain to fail. Most of us know that positive relationships enhance our work, whereas negative relationships strongly influence our desire to leave a school. The quality of relationships built up over the years determines the success of the principal and the school itself. Bryk and Schneider (2002) state that "when an individual sustains a relationship with some person or organization, these long-term social connections can take on value unto themselves.... Individuals come to define themselves as connected to that person or organization" (p. 15). These "long-term social connections" are resilient, and promoting positive relationships among these connections is a major challenge principals face as they lead schools.

In this chapter, we discuss how the concepts of human and social capital are essential to understanding why building positive relationships can be beneficial for the school, the school's mission, and the principal. Then, we offer practical strategies for principals to conduct self-study activities in order to gather information about the existing human and social resources and how best to use and build on those resources. Next we provide suggested activities that principals can use in building relationships—teachers with teachers and principals with teachers. We close the chapter by addressing the inevitable conflict that will occur regardless of the efforts put into building positive relationships.

Investing in Teacher Leadership to Build Human and Social Capital

Principals can lead, but others must agree to follow; this is the essence of leadership. Teachers decide whether to follow their principals or not based on how they act. Their perceptions are influenced by the leader's "capital." Like the business community, where capital is related to money that is available to generate more money, there are four types of capital which leaders use to influence followers:

- Human capital—skills, knowledge and expertise.
- Cultural capital—ways of being.
- Social capital—networks, relations of trust.
- Economic capital—material resources. (Spillane, Hallett, & Diamond, 2003, pp. 3–4)

Principals utilize these forms of capital in their daily interactions with teachers. To build teacher leadership, it is necessary to tap into the existing resources, or capital, teachers already possess. We addressed cultural capital in Chapter 3 when we discussed teachers' adult growth and development. Teachers have minimal access to economic capital; therefore, in this section we will look at human capital and social capital.

Potential for gaining adult human capital through increased social capital in a school resides with the teachers individually and collectively. Coleman (1988) defines human capital as "changes in persons that bring about skills and capabilities that make them able to act in new ways" (p. 100) and says that social capital "exists in the relations among persons" (pp. 100–101). However, like other forms of capital, whether it is maximized or not will depend on how it is managed. Teachers' competence in their classrooms and their chosen social contacts are valuable resources. Left alone, these human and social resources remain virtually unavailable to the school. Bryk and Schneider (2002) found in their study of effective schools that "the arrangement of social exchanges is an important consideration in the overall productivity of any organization, [but] these concerns take on a heightened salience for schools. The social relations of schooling are not just a mechanism of production but they are a valued outcome in their own right" (p. 19). By being aware of teachers' knowledge, interests, talents, and skills, as well as the social networks in which teachers influence others, a principal can purposely structure connections to increase value. Relationships can be encouraged among teachers as well as between teachers and principals to add value to the entire organization. Although many principals use this process intuitively, it is often unsystematic and may result in overlooked teacher leadership potential.

Self-Study: Potential for Increasing Human and Social Capital

See
Tool 4.1
Page 91.

A self-study of human and social capital includes three steps. First, information about the knowledge, interests, talents, and skills of individual teachers, as well as information about the social connections of these teachers should be gathered. Next, there must be an analysis of the existing relationships to determine if they add value to the school and if there are opportunities that could be created to increase value to the organization. Based on this information, principals can build structures in which positive social networks may develop and thrive, thus increasing social capital. Moreover, principals can see where there are dysfunctional relationships that decrease social capital and take steps to minimize their effect. The size of a school will determine the amount of time a principal can devote to the activities suggested in this section. In some cases, a principal may deal with only a section of the teacher population. This is a new approach to looking at personnel, and we encourage principals to meet the challenge of using these tools, because in many cases this proactive strategy will pay off by actually saving time dealing with relationship issues in the future.

Gathering Information

It is important to look for information that reflects the strengths of the teachers rather than focusing on weaknesses. People build on their strengths more readily than they respond to instructions to correct their weaknesses. What a principal may consider a teacher's weakness may end up being a strength with other people. To make good use of human and social capital, principals decide what information is needed and then collect, organize, and analyze the data in ways that are useful to them.

What Information Is Needed?

The purpose of collecting information about teachers is not to select teacher leaders, but to recognize existing and potential teacher leadership.

Even those who are veteran principals and believe teacher leadership is a desired goal must make as few assumptions as possible regarding what human and social capital exist. When principals have been in a school or position for a period of time, they sometimes think that they know all that there is to know about their school. It will be important to suspend those assumptions as much as possible and begin with a fresh and as yet unformed perspective. This information will provide new perspectives, perhaps dispel inaccurate assumptions, and even spark new respect for the accomplishments and interests of individual teachers. Some examples of information principals might seek include the following:

Human Capital

- Evidence of exemplary student learning
- Committee and project lists for the last few years, noting who chaired these committees
- Staff development records to find out who participated and who used the new knowledge and skills
- Honors and awards for teaching, scholarship, and service that reflect leadership

Social Capital

- Teachers who socialize, learn, or volunteer to work with certain other teachers
- Civic and professional association service where leadership is exhibited outside the school
- The school's teacher of the year, if selected by other teachers

Where Is the Information?

Reviewing documents, conducting individual interviews, and observing interactions are critical in providing information for addressing the questions of what knowledge, interests, talents, and skills are present and what relationships already exist?

Search Documents

Principals should access information that already exists before trying to generate new information. Personnel files often have important information regarding teachers' previous work and educational experiences. Additionally, there may be experiences and interests they had prior to working for the school that are never revealed unless the teachers' backgrounds are reviewed. Too often we overlook the level of decision making many teachers take on in roles they assume in their families and in their communities, such as taking care of ailing parents, maintaining more than one job, or organizing community events.

See
Tool 4.2
Page 92.

Searching through records of school communications, such as faculty meeting minutes and committee assignments, will reveal which teachers are involved in school initiatives as well as which teachers have voluntarily attended staff development opportunities. Looking for names that appear repeatedly, principals will discover faculty members who are involved, are looked to for leadership, and seem to be interested in their professional learning and are therefore prime candidates for involvement in the leadership efforts at a school. These individuals are already leaders, even if informal ones.

Interview Teachers

Individual interviews conducted either throughout the school year or during the summer are additional sources of information. Effective use of questions and listening techniques are the most important skills in this data gathering. Using open-ended and structured questions, such as those in Figure 4.1, generates information useful in identifying the full scope of the resources teachers bring as well as their knowledge of other human and social capital. Open-ended questions are best used with teachers who speak freely; structured questions are helpful when a teacher is more reticent.

Figure 4.1. Interviewing Questions

Open-Ended Questions/Requests	Structured Questions
Tell me about your major responsibilities at the school.	Do you feel your strengths are being well utilized? *Probe:* Why do you say that?
Describe leadership in this school.	Who are the leaders in this school? *Probe:* What criteria did you use to determine that these individuals are leaders? *Probe:* How do they lead?
Is there anything about the school you would change if you could?	What one thing would you change about the school if money were not an issue? *Probe:* How is this different from the way things are now?

Open-Ended Questions/Requests	Structured Questions
What activities, such as sports or volunteer work, are you involved in when you are not at school?	Are you involved in any activities, such as sports or volunteer work, outside the school? *Probe:* Could you give me an example of one of these?
Tell me about work you have done with your colleagues at the school.	Which two or three colleagues would you select to help you with a project? *Probe:* Why did you pick these individuals?
Tell me about your professional learning.	Are you involved in any type of formal professional learning? *Probe:* What would you like to learn?

Observe and Listen

See
Resource 4.1
Page 89.

Information can be discovered by listening to the interactions between and among teachers at committee meetings, faculty functions, and, more likely, in the hallways or by the mailboxes. Staying alert to comments faculty members make regarding such things as colleagues they admire (or not), individuals from whom they have received assistance (or not), or those teachers with whom they have worked on committees or projects can provide important insights about the existing and potential human and social capital. Visiting with teachers who are on duty and listening to what they have to say about students can also be enlightening. More directly, observe faculty members teaching in their classrooms. Most school systems require observations in order to meet the formal evaluation obligations, but a reliable source of information is the informal "walk-through" that takes place for short periods, occurs unannounced, and happens frequently throughout the school year. Principals who spend time in classrooms can quickly identify which teachers are leaders or have the potential for leadership.

Using documents, interviews, and observations can help principals begin to develop a picture of teacher leadership potential. Depending on the size of the school and the time available, adjustments in what information to gather and how to gather the information will need to be made. Additionally, principals should be alert to times when there is a lapse in a teacher's leadership, possibly due to outside commitments such as family obligations or a return to graduate school. Perhaps a teacher may need time to "heal" from an earlier leadership experience that was frustrating. Principals need to check out assumptions, ask questions, listen, and analyze the data.

Analysis of the Information Gathered

Data are merely information until meaning is attached. Where is the human capital that adds value? Are existing relationships adding value to the school? Are there relationships that need to be addressed? Are there other relationships that need to be built in order to maximize the potential for change initiatives to succeed? Are there opportunities that could be created to increase value to the organization?

What Relationships Exist?

See
Tool 4.3
Page 37.

Principals now have the baseline data for building teacher leading and learning, just as student achievement and attendance are data for school improvement planning. To facilitate this analysis, the principal can develop a sociogram showing who is connected to whom inside and, if possible, outside the school. Plotting this information in a web, such as the one in Figure 4.2, provides a picture of the human capital and the potential for using social networks to build human capital or improved instruction. Figure 4.2 illustrates the social relationships that existed when Jay arrived as principal of Markham Middle School (described Chapter 2). For example, Teresa, the 7th grade language arts teacher, had social connections with Yolanda, who later became the lead teacher, and with Julie, another language arts teacher. Similarly, Susan is connected to two of the new teachers. Notice how Jaime is linked with Yolanda and Logan, who in turn are socially connected to other teachers. Finally, the marginal teachers network with other teachers who are more successful in their teaching.

The sociogram here is formal and fairly detailed. Again, depending on the size of the school and the time available, principals may need to be more informal. However, even the hand drawing of circles and lines that precipitate the principal's thinking about existing relationships and what they mean in terms of influencing the school will provide important information for future actions.

Figure 4.2. Jay's Initial Sociogram
of Teacher Networks at Markham Middle School

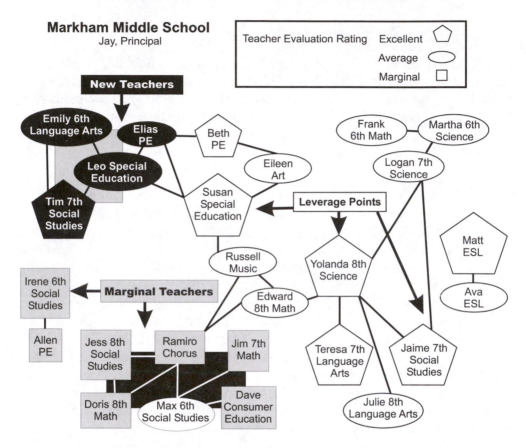

Adapted from Copland, 2001a.

What Existing or Potential Relationships Can Add Value?

Once the sociogram is complete and other information about individual teachers is collected, principals can study the data to determine where value-added relationships exist, where opportunities for value-added relationships could be created, and where there are relationships that are harmful to the school's mission. Connecting the talents of competent teacher leaders who have relationships with teachers who need to improve their skills provides principals with leverage to influence other teachers. For example, in Figure 4.2, Yolanda, Susan, and Jaime, all excellent teachers, are part of social networks that stretch across the school. Jay discovered this during his analysis and saw these individuals as leverage points for influencing other teachers. As Jay purposely built opportunities for teachers to interact, he used this information. On the other hand, understanding the detrimental social networks gives principals the information needed to design strategies that may break down that influence while building other social networks that will help the school.

Principals rely on teacher volunteerism because, other than classroom responsibilities and assigned duties, there are relatively few tasks a principal can mandate. The development of the sociogram and gathering of other information guides the principal to establish conditions in which teachers may desire to volunteer to deal with collective concerns. These data are unique to a school, and they can change as new structures provide opportunities for social networking.

Intentionally Build Positive Relationships

See Resource 4.2 Page 89.

When the data gathering and analysis are completed, it is time to establish opportunities for new positive social networks and relationships. Fullan and Ballew (2004) offer two important points on why the building of positive relationships is essential:

- It's the interactions and relationships among people, not the people themselves that make the difference in organizational success.

- The factor common to every successful change initiated is that relationships improve. If relationships improve, things get better. If relationships remain the same or get worse, ground is lost. (p. 80)

While there can be no guarantee that interactions between and among individuals will be positive, there certainly are steps that can reduce the risks of negative results. A major factor in reducing the risk is for principals to be careful in their actions and use their tacit knowledge of the school as a whole and the knowledge they now have regarding each teacher. The desired outcome of providing opportunities for interaction is to generate what Bryk and Schneider (2002) call "relational trust (that is) forged in daily social exchanges—trust that grows over time through exchanges where the expectations held for others are validated in action" (pp. 136–137).

Building Teacher-with-Teacher Relationships

From the Field I believe you can energize your staff with many things, but without building relationships and a community, the contrived collaboration and/or money spent on a program such as purchasing books for 100 staff members can be wasted.

Lisa N. Mitchell, NBCT
Art Educator and TLN Member
Full-time doctoral student
Greensboro, North Carolina

Teacher-with-teacher relationships are the essence of the school culture. Principals can take actions to build positive relationships by using the human and social capital information they gathered and embedding what they now know about personal and professional issues, described in Chapter 3. Following are six examples of actions principals can take to build positive teacher-with-teacher relationships.

Provide Opportunities for Participation Within Leadership Structures

Within schools are structures that exist or can be created to facilitate the distribution of power and authority throughout the school. Structures may include committees, task forces, or teams in which teachers participate and lead decision making. Inviting and selecting teachers to join in one or more of these structures can enable the social exchanges that build trust.

In most schools there is a core of individuals who either volunteer or are expected to be selected for leadership responsibilities. To include more teachers, the principal can use data collected in the self-study of school relationships. Based on the data collected, they can identify individuals with previously untapped knowledge, interests, skills, and talents, and determine which social networks would be affected or perhaps created with the inclusion of these people. Additionally, the sociogram information may reveal a combination of individuals that should be avoided.

Early on, principals may need to be directive in order to build positive relationships. As the new networks and relationships mature, and teacher leaders emerge, more invitational strategies can be employed and teachers can assume the responsibilities for building schedules and structures that nurture and sustain these positive teacher-with-teacher relationships. We acknowledge the intensity of time needed to accomplish these purposeful decisions; however, principals who keep their eyes on the long-term goal of developing relational trust will find the amount of time needed will decrease as healthy social networks are established.

Build or Use Existing Structures
Where Teachers Lead and Learn Together

When we use the term "structure," our reference is not to buildings or spaces. Rather, we are talking about opportunities, processes, and procedures created to bring teachers together for their learning. Possibilities include the following:

- *Study groups.* These groups can focus on an instructional strategy, analysis of student work, or perhaps a recent book on a topic of importance to student learning needs.

- *Teaching teams.* Teachers who share the same students or teach the same subject can form collaborative groups in which they can share their personal practice in order to improve student learning. The principal's attention to common planning time supports opportunities for team teachers to work with each other.

- *Curriculum development.* Working on curriculum provides a structure where teachers across grade levels and subjects can learn together, as can teachers within grade levels and subjects.

- *Electronic discussion boards.* Teachers who may not share common planning time can be part of a group that meets electronically through discussion boards. Teacher leaders can moderate the discussions, provide resources, and encourage other teachers to share ideas.

Invite Teachers to Travel Together
to Meetings and Conferences

Anyone who has traveled with professional colleagues understands how this can be a strategy for building relationships. Topics that are covered in the hours spent in a car, on a plane, or waiting for the meeting to start often are quite different in kind and depth than the brief encounters within a typical school day. Sharing the experiences of solving problems such as locating the hotel or meeting room, deciding where to go for dinner, and making sure the appropriate materials are packed creates bonds that remain long after the event itself has ended. The trip home provides another opportunity to discuss what was learned, how this might be useful in achieving the school vision, and what actions might be pursued to get started.

Develop Teacher Schedules

See Resource 4.3 Page 90.

Most principals can remember their experiences as teachers and how the colleagues they were mostly likely to know were those with whom they came in contact most frequently, such as teachers in the same grade level, team or department, or subject area. In addition, there are those teachers that became colleagues because they share common duty schedules, lunch periods, or planning periods. Proximity is a powerful tool to use in building relationships between teachers. Giving careful consideration to who is working with whom in a particular schedule can make good use of existing human capital and can generate new social capital as well. Scheduling teaching teams with teachers who are at similar or diverse career phases may create new friendships or impromptu mentor-mentee relationships. Being careful about assigning duties based on information regarding personal obligations will reduce stress for the teachers and increase focus on work during the school day. Taking notice of teachers who are exhibiting early stages of withdrawal, then scheduling them with individuals still fully engaged in their careers might well give these teachers a chance to nurture the other individuals and serve as catalysts for re-engagement.

Plan Social Events

Every school has social events, such as holiday gatherings and beginning- and end-of-the-year socials. These occasions are rich opportunities for building relationships. Principals can organize one or more committees that result in faculty members coming together to work on these events. Providing support by offering space, funds, and communication mechanisms to keep everyone informed will reinforce these developing groups. Occasions for celebration may bring together teachers who might otherwise not know that they share the same birthday month, that they were hired in the same year, or they have children graduating from high school at the same time. These social functions offer new possibilities for the social exchanges necessary in building relational trust.

Restructure Faculty Meetings

See Resources 4.4, 4.5 Page 90.

Much like schedules, faculty meetings are a part of every school year. Because they already exist, making use of them as mechanisms for intentionally building relationships seems obvious. Principals may need part of the agenda to address schoolwide issues, but other items on the agenda can be teacher-planned and teacher-led. Social interaction at the meetings can be purposely designed as well. People generally have a tendency to sit with individuals they already know. This limits the opportunities to get to know individuals outside their groups. Principals might consider asking different teachers to generate schemes for mixing up traditional seating:

- Sitting together by birthday month
- Sitting together according to favorite type of vacation
- Sitting together by family member sequence (all of the only children together, oldest children, youngest children)

Once in new groups, conversation starters can be provided to initiate limited informal exchanges at the beginning of the meeting; teachers can then return to their usual seats before the meeting proceeds.

Another strategy that focuses on school issues invites teachers within an existing group to divide and visit with other groups, then return to their home groups and report on the thinking on issues from other colleagues.

Building Principal-with-Teacher Relationships

Both teachers and principals are dependent on their mutual relationships. Principals depend on teachers to do what is best for students and the school; teachers rely on the principals and other formal leaders not to be unfair. The relationships the principals have with teachers are crucial in building teacher leading and learning. In this section, we offer strategies for building principal-with-teacher relationships.

Become Knowledgeable About Teaching and Learning

From the Field   So then we made lesson plans and I put an assistant principal in each one of their [English teachers'] classrooms full time. The only time (the) assistant principals had off were the ninety minutes that the teachers had off....(The) teachers in the beginning were like, "You are going to be in my classroom?" I said to them: "Yes, but you know what, we are good people. We want to be in there when our test scores go up and we want to be a part of that."

It only took a couple of times for us to be in there that they realized, yeah, they are not here to criticize; they are here to help. We had no discipline problems, and we scored 90 percent and above in every part of the writing. Those kids worked hard.

Aurora Hurtado
Former Principal,
Galena Park Middle School
Galena Park, Texas

Principals who are knowledgeable about teaching and learning build closer relationships with teachers, because teachers relate better to principals who know the work of the schools. Rather than a "hands-off" approach to curriculum and instruction, these principals assume responsibility for knowing what instruction is taking place and for bringing the right people together to solve instructional problems.

Being honest about their knowledge of curriculum and instruction is an important self-assessment for principals, because teachers can easily determine if principals are only pretending to know. Regardless of their teaching backgrounds, principals should know or be willing to learn about effective teaching. The best people to learn from and with are accomplished teachers. Most people do not mind if the principal does not have all the knowledge and skills, as long as he or she is willing to learn.

Visit Meetings and Planning Sessions of Various Groups and Project Teams

Just as there are "walk-throughs" for classroom observations, we advocate "stop-bys" as a strategy for building relationships. Principals are unable to attend every scheduled meeting. However, they can, with a little planning, "stop by" to check in on how things are going with most meetings. Finding time to stop by accomplishes at least three things. First, the principal's presence signals that the work being done is important, and teachers perceive this as an acknowledgment that their efforts are being recognized and appreciated. Second, it allows principals to be in tune with what's going on and who is involved with what's going on. As brief as stop-bys might be, they still provide an opportunity to gather information about the focus of the meeting and the participants. Finally, something learned during a visit could later generate a question from the principal to a teacher in the project, such as, "Were you able to get that draft completed at your meeting yesterday?" or "Is there anything I can do to help you with the schedule for that activity?" These actions of support help build relationships. There may also be an opportunity to connect two or more groups based on information gathered to build new networks of positive relationships.

Use Questioning and Listening Skills

Principals are accustomed to speaking in many settings. What is believed to be an efficient strategy, that is, to give solutions to problems, contributes to the dependency relationship between the principal and teachers. Principals can use questioning and listening skills to help teachers solve their own problems. Probing questions get to the real issues involved, and the principal can use specific types of questions depending on the situation:

- Getting specific information: Can you clarify that?
- Tuning in to others: What do you think about that?

- Getting feedback from others: Did I understand you correctly when you said…?
- Giving feedback to others: What type of feedback would be most helpful to you?
- Closing: Are we in agreement?
- Consequences: What might the long-term results be? (Leeds, 2000, pp. 273–280)

From the Field   My principal came to be an administrator by way of being a coach…. But what makes him different… is that he has his hand on the pulse of our school. He listens better than any administrator I have worked with, and above all he has an abiding desire to do what is best for students.

Jim Brooks, NBCT
AYA English/Language Arts Teacher,
TLN Member
Millers Creek, North Carolina

Listening is an essential skill for leadership, but it is rarely taught. Too many of us believe that we listen better than we actually do. This is the skill most frequently identified by teachers when describing effective principals (Moller et al., 2000). These principals are intense listeners and know how to ask the right questions to get at the problems a teacher is experiencing. Effective principal listening skills include the following:

- Does not appear to be in a hurry
- Talks about a specific aspect of the teacher's work
- Makes eye contact rather than being distracted
- Allows the teacher to finish speaking and pauses to ensure the teacher is finished before speaking
- Makes brief comments and stays focused on the issue rather than trying to handle several issues at the same time
- Sits or stands so that there are minimal distractions
- Avoids sharing a similar experience the principal had and how it was solved

Listen, ask questions, listen, ask questions—this represents the ideal rhythm of interaction when a principal is working with teachers to solve problems.

Provide Human and Fiscal Resources

> **From the Field**   We are high-tech and the technology is finally streamlining some of those routine jobs that eat up teacher time. This year my class sizes are much smaller and there is adequate time to collaborate with colleagues via e-mail and in a workroom conducive to sharing. The administration has been very responsive to requests for supplies and support. No clerical duties.
>
> *Mary K. Tedrow*, NBCT
> Secondary English/Journalism Teacher,
> TLN Member
> Winchester, Virginia

Resources are not limited to dollars, but include personnel, time, space, talent, ideas, and more. While the resources may be expended individually, it is the collective allocation and use of these resources that fuel the operation of the organization. The matching of resources with teachers' needs is one of the principal's primary responsibilities and can be used to build relationships, such as when a principal recognizes teachers' needs even before they ask for resources. Decisions about resources must be driven by the school's vision for student learning, but the vision is accomplished through individual teachers' efforts. Effective principals use all available resources and constantly seek additional sources of support for teachers. Although principals should be fiscally responsible, they can learn to balance fiscal responsibility with generosity to teachers.

Give Extra Attention to New Teachers

The culture of the school is built through relationships. New teachers are acculturated through their relationships with other teachers and with the principal. To sustain a culture of change that supports teacher leading and learning, principals cannot ignore building relationships with new teachers.

The time a principal spends with new teachers reaps payoffs in four ways. First, principals learn more about the individual human and social resources the teacher brings to the school. Second, principals can provide additional materials, equipment, and other support that new teachers do not know how to access. Third, the potential for teacher leadership from new teachers may become evident. Finally, teachers stay in schools where they are supported by the administration, and a principal's investment in building relationships can prevent attrition of talented teachers, whereas on the other hand, these contacts also can identify teachers who are not able to meet the school's expectations.

Be Accessible

Teachers judge whether or not a principal is accessible by the way the principal's time is allocated. Finding the time to meet the paperwork requirements of the job as well as interact with others is one of the most difficult time management problems a principal faces. There are no easy solutions for this, but principals can begin by sharing this concern with faculty and staff, then finding ways to delegate as much administrative paperwork as possible. In understaffed schools, this may be difficult, but it may surprise the principal who might be willing to take on reports that before were considered the responsibility of the principal.

Match Individual Interests with School-Site Opportunities

From the Field I am fortunate to work with an administrator who is positively gifted in her ability to discern potential leadership…. She has an uncanny knack for saying to a teacher, "You know, you should consider (insert here anything from 'going for National Board certification' to 'taking a Lead Teacher course')," and she is NEVER wrong….

Gail V. Ritchie, NBCT
Resource Teacher, TLN Member
Fairfax, Virginia

Thinking about individual teachers, rather than about teachers as a whole group, is a unique talent. Ever-watchful principals can determine individual teachers' interests and attempt to match these with opportunities. What appeals to one teacher may not appeal to another, so principals are wise to consider individual differences as they seek ways to encourage teachers' growth and development. If teachers are provided a variety of options, like food on a buffet, there will be some teachers who step up to certain invitations and others who find different options attractive. Lovely (2005) stresses the importance of building on teachers' interests and strengths:

> Teacher leaders need to be cultivated in accordance with their talents and interests. Finding tasks that suit each individual best allows every member of a faculty to experience a sense of accomplishment. (p. 18)

Encourage Teachers' Involvement in School System, Regional, and State Projects

Principals are often asked to nominate, recommend, or appoint representatives to projects initiated by the school system. Regional agencies, such as educational service centers, school study councils, leadership consortia, and other networks may also have need for teacher participation. Similarly, though not as frequently, state organizations such as state departments, professional associations, state-level commissions, and task forces will request that principals suggest teachers to be invited for service. When asked, principals should have in mind the school's human and social resources in order to provide opportunities to individuals that may be an especially good fit for the activity. Participation in these experiences gives teachers a chance to lead by serving as a liaison between school and school system. Principals need to be proactive in promoting teachers for these opportunities.

Avoid Possessive Language

Often principals use possessive language such as "my teachers" or "my school." The use of this language sends a subtle message to teachers that the principal is in control and they are merely players in the principal's master plan. Of course, most principals do not feel this way, but the language contradicts efforts to build collaboration. Instead principals should use language that is inclusive, such as "we," "our," and "us."

Attend Professional Learning Activities with Teachers

From the Field I knew my principal and other faculty members were interested in updating instructional strategies for reading, so I invited my principal to attend this four-day institute with me. We drove the 70-mile one-way trip together. For four days, our conversation centered on what we had learned and our plans for the coming school year.

Vickie Brockman, NBCT
Fourth Grade Teacher,
TLN Member
Clover, South Carolina

One of the most important roles principals play in supporting and nurturing professional learning is participating as active colearners with the teachers. Principals cannot participate in every professional learning experience, but they must be active learners in the school's primary initiatives. When principals do not attend, it sends a clear message to the teachers that the learning is not important. There is a growing trend in school systems to require principals to participate in order for teachers to be included in a professional learning program.

Attend Teacher-Planned Social Events

The social events discussed earlier in building teacher relationships can also be sources for building relationships between principals and teachers. Principals may discover this provides opportunities for them to observe who interacts with whom, who is leading and managing the activities, and how problems are solved when they occur. These events are laboratories for observing teacher leadership. Also, attending teacher planned social events allows the principal to be viewed in a different role. While never completely eliminated, the power and authority of the position are minimized during these events, allowing conversations between teachers and the principal that may never occur in more formal work settings.

There will be events in teachers' personal lives when it would be appropriate for principals to support them. For example, a personal illness, the marriage of a child, or the loss of a family member can be stressful and pull a teacher from full attention on his or her professional work. The principal's actions could include offering classroom support at the school, attending events, or simply writing a note to the teacher that acknowledges the stress the teacher is experiencing.

Share Information About Personal Interests

Principals and other administrators often try to separate their professional and personal interests, especially when they are interacting with people they supervise. The causes for partitioning one's life are numerous, but a commonly cited reason is a concern about stepping beyond the typical boss-subordinate relationship. Administrators are socialized into the culture of their work, just as teachers are taught how to act within the teaching culture. Fishbein and Osterman (2001) found that administrative interns were taught by their mentors to protect themselves, while teachers also tended to protect themselves from administrators.

Principals who want to improve relationships with teachers are willing to share of themselves, including personal information. If teachers see the principal as a person who balances professional and personal commitments, they will believe that the principal will understand their unpredictable personal situations. In addition, as principals, teachers, and other staff members share about themselves, there will be common areas of interest that can promote relationships. The boundaries of professional relationships can be maintained even when principals let other people know about themselves.

Follow Through Consistently

The act of following through on commitments seems obvious to most people, but with the busy lives of principals there is tendency to put off, forget, or ignore these commitments. A principal's ability to follow through is an indicator to teachers of how well the principal listens to them, and it builds trust by assuming responsibility for actions agreed upon.

Principals may sometimes feel overwhelmed, but teachers are watching to see if there is follow-up on commitments, especially if the action relates to them personally. A principal who makes promises to teachers and does not follow up on them damages relationships. To avoid forgetting a promise made to a teacher, principals should find ways to keep track of these promises. Many principals have developed their own strategies for avoiding this problem such as PDAs or even pocket notepads.

Provide Genuine Recognition

See
Tool 4.4
Page 95.

We are amazed as we work with teacher leaders to hear about the absence of recognition even when they accomplish extraordinary tasks. Most teachers do not seek elaborate forms of recognition, especially in front of their peers, but they do crave even small indications that they are doing a good job. A simple note from the principal placed in a teacher leader's mailbox will be saved for months or even years. Of course, teachers, like students, do not respond as well to general praise as they do when the principal cites a behavior the teacher exhibited. As teacher leadership grows, there will be more willingness from teachers to accept public praise from the principal and other teachers. The principal can move away from providing all the recognition by encouraging teachers to give recognition to each other.

From the Field   My new principal started a "staff member of the month"… The winner is drawn from all the nominees and wins something like a gift certificate or $25. I hate these things; even though it's determined by a drawing, it's still competitive in my mind, and not a morale booster. Why can't we encourage collaboration?

Cathy Kinzler, NBCT
Library Media Specialist, TLN Member
Richmond, Virginia

From the Field   But it is the informal recognition that we get that means more….I can't think of a day this year where the principal or assistant principals didn't thank me for being at this school. I can't think of a day where they didn't engage me in conversation as a colleague rather than a subordinate.

Bill Ferriter, NBCT
Sixth Grade Language Arts/Social Studies, TLN Member
Raleigh, North Carolina

Conflict Is Inevitable

See
Resource 4.6
Page 90.

Nurturing a professional learning community is difficult work for a number of reasons, but perhaps the most challenging is dealing with the inevitable conflict. The predictable changes in teaching staffs due to ongoing attrition of teachers and the principals' limited authority to select replacement teachers result in a mix of viewpoints. Diverse perspectives are seldom explored because there are few opportunities for teachers to learn about each other except in pockets of friendships that develop among like-minded teachers. Most of us like to work in harmony with others; however, in a genuine professional learning community where the conversations go beyond congeniality to discuss what is valued most by teachers—their teaching and students—there will be conflict. Principals have an obligation to help people embrace these differences in productive ways. This obligation brings us back to the primary purpose for building teacher leadership within a learning community, which is to build a democratic workplace where the shared values allow for the expression of different perspectives from individuals and groups.

Dealing with Conflict

The principal's day is filled with conflict that involves students, parents, teachers, custodians, bus drivers, secretaries, cafeteria workers, central office personnel, and others. There are many days that principals go home only to realize they accomplished little of what they had planned because they were embroiled in conflict. Teachers, however, are often inducted into a culture that expects little or no expression of disagreement and at least an appearance that collegiality pervades all interactions. Most teachers are in unique situations where there are options for not working together, avoiding conflict, and therefore not moving beyond the issue. To move beyond this escape route, principals and teachers need to work in safe structures, or "holding environments to contain and adjust the heat that is being generated by addressing difficult issues or wide value differences" (Heifetz & Linsky, 2002, p. 102).

A strategy to prepare faculty and staff in their dealings with conflict is to engage them in building a common language around the issue of conflict. When people use the same words for emotionally laden experiences, it helps to defuse the situation. Providing safety for public discussions of differences and skillfully managing conflict is essential; if conflict is handled poorly, it will affect the school culture and stall improvement efforts. There are three ways to deal with conflict:

- *Avoid dealing with conflict.* This strategy is selected too often because people do not want to be upset or do not have the skills to confront or collaborate to manage conflict. Still, there are times when it is wise to avoid conflict because confronting it may only make the situation worse, or the time might not be right for dealing with the issue.

- *Confront conflict.* There are situations in which a person must stand up for what they believe and defend a position, but teachers are not often willing to do this because they know that silence is safer in the teaching community. Principals may need to bring conflict to the surface without trying to solve the problem. This may require encouraging people with eccentric ideas or those who have an opposing view to speak out. If used with skill, confrontation can result in a compromise that is achievable.

- *Collaborate to manage conflict.* A compromise that may come out of confronting conflict may result in unequal satisfaction among the people involved. Collaboration, though, works to find mutual agreement that is acceptable to everyone. This strategy takes more time and requires the people involved to explore each other's interests, needs, and perspectives. At first, principals can facilitate collaborative management of conflict, but in time, teachers must learn the skills and help each other work together to find creative solutions.

Principals and teachers can be proactive in learning skills to handle conflict in their work with each other. Ignoring this important interpersonal skill development can result in unplanned chaos throughout the school that may spill out into the community.

Summary

Leadership is all about relationships. Yet when aspiring principals go through many graduate programs, there is relatively little emphasis on the importance of the skills needed to build relationships. Although they study human resource management, potential principals rarely learn how to build a professional learning community. Through personal experiences, usually on the job, principals learn the hard way how neglecting the building of relationships makes a difference in the ways that schools respond to diverse students, accountability demands, and community pressure. We believe that collective action to address student learning cannot happen without purposeful actions on the part of the principal to build positive relationships.

Teacher leadership can result in increased human and social capital focused on student learning. After completing a self-study of the existing human and social resources, we recommend that principals intentionally build social networks. As relationships change and become more fluid, there will be conflict, which principals and teacher leaders must acknowledge, honor, and work to manage. The conflicts are predictable, but when principals understand this and have the skills to be constructive in their handling of interpersonal issues, there is hope for teacher leadership to emerge and grow.

Principals can use the Intentional Leadership Rubric for Positive Relationships (Figure 4.1) to determine their current skills.

Figure 4.3. Positive Relationships Rubric

	Quality teacher leadership requires essential positive relationships.
Unsure & Unskilled	Teachers are known to the principal and to each other; some self-selected groups are intact. Everyone is cordial, but limited in their interactions with each other.
Moving Along	Teachers' talents, skills, and interests, as well as their social networks are known to the principal; the number of purposefully established groups has increased and most teachers are participating in one or more school structures.
Leading Teacher Leaders	Teachers' talents, skills, and interests, as well as their social networks are known to the principal and to other teachers; groups are established voluntarily, by invitation, and by assignment; the principal, teacher leaders, and teachers themselves take the initiative to link individuals together in realizing the school vision.

If principals intentionally build trust through positive relationships, they can then turn their attention to establishing structures for distributing power and authority. Before starting, though, it is important for principals to be clear about their beliefs and values regarding distributing power and authority. Unless principals are firm in their commitment for this move to a new way of leading and learning, any actions will be perceived as contrived and will violate trust with the teachers. Once the decision is made, there are specific leadership actions that will ensure that the effort will be worthwhile.

Resources

4.1 Ginsberg, M. B., & Murphy, D. (2002). How walkthroughs open doors. *Educational Leadership, 59*(8), 34–36—The authors describe benefits and procedures for walkthroughs.

4.2 Brewster, C., & Railsback, J. (2003). *Building trusting relationships for school improvement: Implications for principals and teachers.* Portland, OR: Northwest Regional Educational Laboratory—The authors describe the importance of trust and how to build relationships between teachers and between the principal and teachers.

on September 26, 2005, from http://www.nwrel.org/request/2003sept/teachers.html

4.3 Schroth, G., Beaty, D., & Dunbar, R. (2003). *School scheduling strategies: New ways of finding time for students and staff.* Lancaster, PA: ProActive Publishers—This book is a principal's guide to time-effective, learning-focused scheduling. Each step in the scheduling process is detailed and illustrated with practical examples.

4.4 Calabrese, R. L., Short, G., & Zepeda, S. J. (1996). *Hands-on leadership tools for principals.* Larchmont, NY: Eye on Education—The authors provide practical suggestions for effective faculty meetings (pp. 12–17).

4.5 Robbins, P., & Alvy, H. B. (1995). *The principal's companion: Strategies and hints to make the job easier.* Thousand Oaks, CA: Corwin—The authors offer strategies to align the school's mission with faculty meetings (pp. 172–181).

4.6 Webne-Behrman, H. (n.d.). Conflict Resolution website—Provides information about conflict, common problems in dealing with conflict, and eight steps to resolve conflict. Retrieved on September 25, 2005, from http://www.ohrd.wisc.edu/onlinetraining/resolution/index.asp

Tools

4.1 Common Characteristics of Teacher Leaders

Step 1: Identify a teacher leader you know:

_____

Step 2: Write down three to five descriptors that tell why you selected this teacher.

Step 3: Compare the descriptors you selected with the four categories displayed in the chart below.

Common Characteristics of Teacher Leaders			
Interpersonal Skills	**Professional Expertise**	**Focus on Students**	**Leadership**
Enthusiastic	Up-to-date	Advocates for children	Takes risks
Has integrity	Committed to the improvement of teaching & learning	Involves parents	Is outspoken
Reflective	Promotes the profession	Pays attention to student needs	Embraces/ initiates change
Shares weaknesses	Lifelong learner	Has high expectations	Sees the "big picture"
Collaborates	Excellent teacher	Seeks resources	Stops by other teachers' classrooms to help out
Consensus builder	Expertise in content	Attends student events	Visionary
Earns trust of teachers	Mentor	Cares about students	Team player

Step 4: Answer these questions:
- Did the characteristics of the teacher leader you selected match the pattern of characteristics of teacher leaders?
- Did the words selected fall into one of these four categories: interpersonal skills, professional expertise, focus on students, and leadership?

Step 5: Use this information as you conduct a self-study of human and social resources.

Tool 4.2   Teacher Leader Information

Listed below are suggestions for the types of information to gather. Following this list is a table that demonstrates one way this information could be recorded. Principals are encouraged to develop ways to organize that best suit their situations. The table not only aids in gathering the information for each individual but also allows comparisons and category groups.

Sample Areas of Information to Collect

- Teacher's career history, such as when they started working, whether they have always been at this school, or whether they have taught other grades or subjects
- Years of teaching experience
- Formal education (undergraduate, master's degree, master's degree plus additional coursework, doctorate)
- Major study areas for each degree
- Special areas of interest or talent, such as special collections of items or documents, writing, musical, dance or theater interests, carpentry, crafts
- National Board Certification for Teachers or other special certificates
- Awards for teaching or service work in the school or in the community
- Appearance of names in handbooks, meeting minutes, or other documents as a leader of any school committees
- Name attached to any particular projects
- Recent professional learning experiences
- Membership in any civic associations and role played
- Other information

Figure 4.4. Chart of Information Collected

	Natasha Kdg	Antonio Kdg	Vincent 5th	Susan 5th	Judy 1st	Gary 1st	Mike 1st	Ava 2nd	Aidee 2nd
Career history?									
Years of experience?									
Degrees & major areas of study?									
Awards?									
Community work?									
Involved in committees?									
Hobbies or outside interests?									

Tool 4.3   Develop a Sociogram
Representing Relationships in Your School

Being explicit in determining the existing human and social resources is helpful in planning strategies for creating social networks and supporting or changing existing social networks. Follow these steps to develop a sociogram for your school:

Step 1: Study the sociogram in Figure 4.2 (page 74) representing the teachers at Markham Middle School.

Step 2: Based on the information gathered through interviews, observations, and documents, draft a sociogram of your school's faculty regarding the competence level of the teachers and their social networks.

Step 3: Once the sociogram is complete, study these data by asking questions such as the following:

- Does the sociogram represent the staff's interactions? If it does not, what areas are misrepresented?
- Has everyone been included?
- Do some individuals have multiple networks? Is there any pattern as to which networks include these individuals?
- Are there clusters of isolated "interacters"?
- Are there any individuals in these isolated clusters that might become leaders to connect with other networks?
- Do all members of the clusters represented have beliefs aligned with the school's shared vision? If not, what beliefs do they hold?
- Who are the key influencers in each cluster?
- Are there any individuals who are key influencers in more than one cluster?

Tool 4.4   Suggestions for Recognizing Teachers

- *Public recognition.* At meetings, recognize not individual teachers but team efforts. Use public recognition sparingly, because even teams of teachers can experience rejection from other teachers if others believe the recognition sends a message that they must change.

- *Private notes.* Place a private note in the teacher's mailbox as close as possible to the time when the teacher leader accomplished a task. This recognition is private, and teachers can choose to share it or not.

- *Funding.* Encourage the leadership team responsible for professional development funding to allocate resources for a teacher leader to attend a professional conference.

- *Media.* Use a variety of media to share the successes of teacher leaders. These may include newsletters, articles in local newspapers, and other strategies.

- *Award symbols.* Create an award symbol from an ordinary object. For example, award a green felt-tip pen. Be sure that the individual knows that this is a special recognition; not everyone gets a green pen. It will not be too long and teachers will be talking about the green pens and how they were earned.

- *Theme items.* There are a number of companies and office supply stores that carry all sorts of supplies such as paper, bookmarks, or pins with congratulatory or affirming statements. If the school has a theme for the year, this could be a way to provide recognition.

- *Postcards.* Send positive message postcards through the U.S. mail to teachers' homes.

- *Books.* Teachers generally love books—of all sorts! A book that focuses on such issues as classroom activities, poetry, or letters to teachers will be welcomed.

- *Candy.* Give a piece or small box of candy. Find clever ways to play off the names of candy, such as Payday, $100,000 Bar, or Life Savers.

- *Time.* Everyone needs more time. Offering to teach a class for a teacher leader who has completed a major task is always a welcome reward.

- *Seek out ideas.* Use resources to find recognition ideas, such as *You Made My Day: Creating Co-Worker Recognition & Relationships,* by J. Allen and M. McCarthy (New York: Lebhar-Friedman Books, 2000).

5

Distributing Power and Authority

A comment made by many leaders is, "It would be easier if I did it myself." We agree that in many cases this is true, but distributing power and authority is not just about making the principal's work more manageable, it is about building teachers' leadership capacity so that, over time, the school's initiatives can be self-sustaining and not dependent on a single leader or a small group of leaders.

This chapter provides principals with an overview of four reasons why they might want to distribute power and authority. Then actions are suggested that will help principals examine their beliefs about relinquishing power and authority. Next, we recommend ways to intentionally build and sustain a system that supports teachers as they take on leadership roles. Finally, we look at structures that foster collaborative leadership.

Reasons to Distribute Power and Authority

See Resource 5.1 Page 115. The first reason to distribute power and authority is to break the bonds of dependence between the principal and the teachers. In schools, there is a tendency for those who do not have authority to expect to have their needs satisfied by those who do. Conversely, principals may choose to satisfy their own needs by being caretakers rather than helping teachers become self-initiating and self-managing problem solvers.

As the dependency relationship decreases, the workload becomes more manageable for the principal and leadership can move beyond one person. Principals have to acknowledge these emotional needs and build structures and experiences to move toward collaborative leadership. If teachers always seek approval and permission from the principal, it is impossible to have a democratic workplace. The driver of decisions and actions must be an articulated, shared vision rather than permission from any one person.

A second reason for distributing power and authority is to build leadership throughout the school so that improvements are not totally dependent on the person who sits in the principal's chair. The "hero leader" is a liability that denies teachers responsibility for learning, leading, and sustaining continuous improvement long beyond the tenure of any one principal. An increase in teacher leadership buffers the predictable turnover of principals with a critical mass of teacher leaders who can ensure that improvement efforts are continued. Distributing power and authority moves principals from struggling with the unrealistic expectations that they are the sole instructional leaders, but it also requires them to take responsibility for building communities of leaders and learners.

The third reason for distributing power and authority is to increase leadership resources. Many principals begin their tenure believing that they must fulfill every leadership demand placed on them or others will view them as incompetent. It is not long before principals realize they cannot be "all things to all people," so they must make choices about how they will cope with these responsibilities. Rather than feeling guilty about not meeting every expectation, we encourage principals to consider a perspective that sees power and authority as tools for expanding leadership. Principals who hold this view believe that power is infinite rather than finite. They find ways to involve as many leaders as possible, resulting in service to students that one person could never envision.

Finally, our fourth reason for wanting the hero myth to die out is that it is detrimental not only to the school but also to the principal. Heifetz and Linsky (2002) go so far as to say "the lone warrior myth of leadership is a sure route to heroic suicide" (p. 100). Trying to move a vision forward alone can result in "marginalization" (Heifetz & Linsky, 2002, p. 32) that puts the principal on the fringe of the professional school community and makes this person a target for conflict.

Even when principals express a desire to distribute power and authority, they have concerns about teachers who are unwilling to accept the burden of leadership. It is true that not all teachers welcome invitations to be leaders; this reluctance may be nested in behaviors and attitudes that have been in the making for a long time or based on their relationships with principals who believed they needed to be in control of everything. Granted, teachers cannot be empowered without accepting the power; on the other hand, principals can work to develop a school culture where teachers believe that they will be authentically engaged in leadership. Eventually, principals can selectively give up control, trust others to be responsible for their leadership, and in time, watch teachers as they become self-organizing in their leadership.

Acting on the belief that power can lead to more power is risky and requires courage from the principal, but it can result in unlimited opportunities for the school. However, the first decision principals must make is whether or not they are willing to share power and authority. This decision must be based on the principal's personal belief about collaboratively working with teachers. The next section gives principals an opportunity to explore their beliefs and their willingness to move in this direction.

Self-Study:
Beliefs About Distributed Power and Authority

If the hesitation to distribute power and authority by the principal and, in turn, the reluctance of the teachers to accept it is to be resolved, both teachers and principals must begin to view power and authority as a shared commodity. While it would be ideal if everyone could come to this recognition simultaneously, it is the principal who must take the first steps.

If principals view power as fixed in the position of principal, then distributing power and authority is anathema to them. On the other hand, if principals view power and authority as resources to be shared, distributing them becomes a way to increase power both organizationally and individually. Principals can start by being honest with themselves about their personal beliefs regarding the distribution of power and authority. Teachers are quick to discern what the principal sincerely believes. Starting on the path to support an endeavor in which the principal has little or no confidence is at best a façade and perhaps more realistically a ruse—not a good context in which to develop trust and teacher leadership.

Examining Beliefs About Distributing Power and Authority

To examine their beliefs, principals can reflect on their personal experiences, acknowledge the risks, and examine what is known about collaborative leadership. Then they can make a decision about whether or not they are willing to commit to distributing power and authority. If they do commit to this, then we recommend that they write a personal vision statement to guide their actions.

Reflect on Personal Experiences as a Teacher Leader

See Tool 5.1 Page 115.

One strategy principals can use to assess the strength of their beliefs in teacher leadership is to reflect on their experiences as teachers. Individuals in formal leadership positions generally exhibit leadership, both formal and informal, throughout their lives. With personal initiative and the support of other people, most principals develop leadership skills in order to reach their goals and survive in the context of the school. Although past experiences as a teacher leader help principals recognize the concept, their involvement as teacher leaders may have been haphazard and have taken place in a variety of contexts.

Principals usually start their educational careers as classroom teachers. In order to be considered for a principalship, individuals pursuing this goal must have exhibited leadership to someone who made the decision to move them to the position of principal. Although a graduate degree in educational leadership is a prerequisite in most states, the determining factor in the selection of an individual as principal is often behavior demonstrated through past leadership roles.

To link the concept of teacher leadership to principals' personalized contexts as teacher leaders may be challenging, depending on the number of years they have been in an administrative role. However, most principals can remember their classroom teaching experiences as well as how and when they, as teachers, either formally or informally provided leadership.

Acknowledge Risks
in Distributing Power and Authority

In most cases, principals' understanding of schools is more complex and comprehensive than that of other staff, so principals can foresee problems more easily. Their experiences with conflict and other interpersonal predicaments often make them legitimately hesitant to distribute power, because they know ultimately their supervisors will look to them as being responsible for any decision made. Consequently, principals may have legitimate concerns about distributing power and authority. Cited below are questions principals pose as we talk with them about teacher leadership. Responses to each question will vary depending on the situation, but principals should consider each one.

- Can negative teachers ever become positive teachers?
- Will scheduling collaboration time be viewed positively by the community?
- Can teacher leaders be rewarded without others viewing this as favoritism?
- Will traditional department or team chairs be willing to share power?
- Can the administrative and the teacher leaders' agendas be aligned?
- How can younger, less experienced principals work successfully with veteran teacher leaders?
- What happens if teachers make poor decisions?
- Will I be seen as not doing the job I am being paid for if I share power?
- Will other principals see me as someone to emulate or someone to isolate?

Examine the Knowledge Base
About Distributing Power and Authority

It is often difficult for busy principals to take time for their own learning. A colleague of ours often makes this point with educators by saying, "You can't teach what you don't know any more than you can come back from where you have never been" (James Boyer, personal communication, October 22, 1992). Principals come from their personal experiences as teacher leaders, but they must also be grounded in their knowledge about distributing power and authority.

The following suggestions are offered for helping principals learn the basics about distributed power and authority:

- *Read books or journal articles explaining this concept.* Literature to learn about distributing power and authority is plentiful. Reading in the area of teacher leadership will reveal a variety of terms used to describe this concept (see Figure 5.1).

Figure 5.1. Terms Regarding Distributing Power and Authority

Terms	Sources
Parallel leadership	Crowther, Kaagan, Ferguson, & Hann, 2002
Building leadership capacity	Lambert, 2003
Providing opportunities for leadership	Drago-Severson, 2004
Shared and supportive leadership	Hord, 2004
Distributed leadership	Spillane, Halverson, & Diamond, 2004

- *Visit schools in which teacher leadership is the norm.* Principals can contact staff members in state administrator or teacher professional associations to identify schools with positive reputations regarding teacher leadership. Phone conversations, site visits, and reviews of documents from schools where teacher leadership is common practice can provide important information on the process used and the results attained.

- *Attend professional learning experiences.* Although many central office leaders strive to establish community among principals, in most systems there is competition that inhibits these conversations. Principals can seek like-minded peers at summer institutes or other renewal activities designed to help practicing principals learn from each other about a variety of issues, especially about how to work with teachers to build a community of learners.

Only by knowing what the distribution of power and authority entails can principals have an image of what the concept means for the school. When the image has been formed, principals can knowledgeably compare their personal beliefs with what will most likely happen in practice. At first, principals may not fully embrace teacher leadership—although that would be desirable—but they may, at least, see distributing power and authority with teacher leaders as a possible goal to pursue.

Commit Time and Energy

After reflecting on personal experiences as a teacher leader, acknowledging the possible consequences of distributing power and authority, and examining the knowledge base about the idea, it is time to act. Principals can make the choice to either commit time and energy to pursuing the next stages of increasing teacher leadership or to put distributing power and authority aside and look for another model of leadership that better aligns with their personal beliefs. Without such a level of commitment, moving to strategies for building teacher leadership is ill-advised and doomed to failure.

Write a Personal Vision Statement

See
Tool 5.2
Page 119.

If principals make the commitment to continue, the next step to take is to write a personal vision statement describing how they want distributed leadership and power to play out. A vision statement draws many ideas together into few sentences that provide a focus on the desired way that adults will lead and learn together. This personal vision statement will be a stimulus for the principal's actions that, in turn, will link to the school's shared vision for working together to improve student learning.

When principals are clear in their own minds about how schools can function with distributed power and authority, teachers are more likely to be leaders in countless ways. This written personal vision statement should be revised as the process unfolds; principals can use it as a touchstone when the journey grows tiresome, the complexity of the endeavor is revealed, or the losses seem to outnumber the gains.

Acting to Distribute Power and Authority

This section presents several actions that principals and teachers can take to move forward in distributing power and authority. First is the development of a shared vision that will drive decision making and leadership. Next, we examine ways to support collective decision making and delegation.

Develop Shared Vision for Student Learning

See
Resource 5.2
Page 115.

The school must have a compelling vision that pulls everyone toward its realization. The vision must be embedded in the school culture, and in turn, the culture must support the achievement of the vision. Earlier we recommended that principals write a personal vision statement as part of their self-study for examining their beliefs about distributed power and authority. At this point, principals need to move beyond themselves and facilitate the collective development of a school vision that will guide the decisions and actions of everyone. A vision helps formulate an image of the desired future state regarding school operations for improved student learning. A school vision involves everyone—if not in the development, certainly in the ratification, implementation, and achievement of the vision. The ultimate purpose of all schools—the continuous improvement of learning for all students—must both energize and direct every element of the vision development. Here are three actions to develop a shared vision.

> **From the Field** The former principal of our school, who is my mentor...says, "If you let the management of it all get in the way of creating the vision and making things happen, you'll never get anywhere."
>
> *Michelle Pedigo*
> Middle School Principal
> MiddleWeb Diary

Step 1: Imagine the Ideal School

Record input from participants that best describes the desired future. There could be any number of these statements, depending on the various dimensions needed to describe the ideal. The goal is to get a rich description of every dimension of desired student learning from as many different perspectives as possible.

Step 2: Synthesize the Information

Synthesizing first by category and then into an articulate whole allows the creation of a statement describing the ideal school envisioned by the group. For example the category of literacy might have descriptors such as "all students are literate." The category of professional learning might use words such as "continuous follow-up." Now the task becomes how best to include literacy and professional learning in a statement that most accurately describes the desired future state, such as in this example: "The ideal school will engage in quality professional learning that will result in strategies to ensure all students learn."

Step 3: Share and Use the Vision

Once developed, the vision statement needs to be disseminated to all primary stakeholders, both inside and outside the school. It must also be used at every level of the organization to guide decisions and actions. Principals can model this by specifically referencing the vision at various points in discussions and always asking how a particular decision moves the school toward achieving the vision. For example, if a suggestion is made to adopt a particular program, principals can ask questions such as, "Does this action fit with what we have stated as our vision for this school?" When the principal routinely uses the school vision as a guide for decisions, the professional staff will soon adopt the same strategy when considering decisions on teaching teams, on committees, or in individual classrooms.

Collaborate in Decision Making

From the Field   Very few decisions are made without teacher input. It is not unusual to have the administration put a problem on the table and let the grade level solve it—and you would be amazed at how teachers will step up to the plate and do the unimaginable when given the power!

Dayle Timmons, NBCT
Special Education Teacher,
TLN Member,
2004 Florida Teacher of the Year
Jacksonville, Florida

Relying on others to make decisions or to help with decisions is a reality of today's complex school organizations. Collaborative decision making is easy to say but not necessarily easy to do. Mandates for shared decision making are common, but the reality of sharing this power is in the hands of the principal. Principals who are willing to act democratically reflect their beliefs in supportive and shared leadership (Huffman & Hipp, 2003).

The process of decision making is the core of school administration (Ward & Wilcox, 1999). Decision making is also an important skill for teachers. Teachers must be good decision makers every day in their classrooms as they make hundreds of decisions about time, materials, strategies, discipline, and other classroom-related issues. Yet they are rarely invited to participate in making substantive schoolwide decisions.

Before collaborating on decisions, it is essential to determine who should participate in what parts of the decision-making process. The parameters should identify which decisions are the principal's alone, in what circumstances the group would provide advice to the principal, and when the group would be solely responsible. Too often these discussions take place after the principal and teachers are engaged in sharing decisions, resulting in frustration for the teachers and anxiety for the principal. Lack of clarity on the decision-making parameters may be a source of more frustrations, disappointment, and distrust than any other issue. Too often individuals commit time and energy to share in decisions, make recommendations, and generate solutions only to have their work rejected, modified severely, or not even acknowledged. Participants need to know at the start whether they are giving the principal advice or actually making decisions. If teachers know they are advisory, they can understand when their advice is not taken. But if teachers believe their decisions are to be final and these decisions are ignored, then conflict and disappointment are inevitable.

See Tool 5.3 Page 122.

Four elements should be considered when determining who should be involved in what decisions:

- *Test of relevance (Bridges, 1967).* Most of us do not want to waste our time being involved in decisions about issues that we perceive as irrelevant. So the first "test" is whether or not the teachers have high levels of interest in the decision because they hold a personal stake in it. If they do, then they will have more interest in and want more involvement in decisions in these areas. For example, teachers would most likely consider the adoption of a school reform model as relevant to their work. On the other hand, there may be areas of decision making regarding facility renovation that are not relevant, depending on how they affect the teachers.

- *Test of expertise (Bridges, 1967).* It is possible that teachers may perceive a decision as having relevance to them but have no expertise that would allow them to assist competently in the decision-making process. If there is high interest in the area in which the decision is to be made, then competence must be developed in order to make an effective contribution. For instance, school finance is often a mystery to teachers, but if they believe it is relevant to their involvement in decision making, then the principal can provide training in this area.

- *Test of jurisdiction (Owens, 2001).* Principals are vested with the power and authority to make decisions that by law cannot be delegated to the teachers, even if they have a high interest and expertise in an area such as reappointment of teachers. For those problems that have legal or policy restrictions, individuals can consult the appropriate resources.

- *Test of intensity (Pankake, 1998).* Interest in a particular decision can change depending on the stage of a project. At the beginning of a project, teachers may only want information, but this may change to a desire for direct participation as the project matures. Similarly, projects can require different levels and areas of expertise as they develop. Keeping this developmental perspective in mind helps principals and teacher leaders maintain flexibility regarding the intensity of the involvement.

Once decisions are made regarding the procedures for decision making, they should be reflected in teacher and student handbooks. If a school does not already have handbooks in place, a committee or team to develop them should be created. When these standard operating procedures are developed and disseminated, leadership for solving these issues is distributed throughout the school; recurring decisions can be made appropriately by others, and school leaders can reallocate their time to more strategic decisions.

Delegate Effectively

See
Resource 5.3
Page 115.

As teachers take on responsibilities based on collaborative decision making, the principal relinquishes control and delegates tasks to others. If principals are to create an inclusive model of leadership, effective delegation is a must. Here are seven actions that principals can take to increase the effectiveness of their delegation.

- *Ensure the appropriate people are involved, and communicate their responsibilities to others.* Identifying who should be involved at what

See
Tool 5.4
Page 123.

level and when is part of the planning process. Others need information about to whom authority is being delegated. Failure to do this will create confusion among the staff and undermine the work of the teacher leaders. For instance, the principal needs to refer questions and conversations about projects to the teacher leader to whom the work has been delegated. Updates on various initiatives can be provided during faculty meetings or through written reports by those who are "heading things up." Everyone should know who is responsible for a particular initiative.

- *Communicate the principal's role.* Principals should consult with teacher leaders working on projects to get their views and clearly communicate what roles principals see themselves playing in the projects. This might include agreements such as attendance at meetings or voting privileges. The principal should be able to live with the role agreed upon and follow through with letting go of control. At times, principals' roles will vary depending on the experience of the teacher leaders or the scope of the work. To declare one role and then try to fill another will generate distrust and resentment, leading to a reduced pool of willing volunteers for sharing in the work.

- *Clarify the tasks to be done.* Getting things done will be made much easier if there is a clear understanding of what is to be accomplished. This can best be done by putting the plan in writing. Deciding together what will exist when this work is successfully completed that did not exist before is important at the beginning and becomes even more critical as things get under way. This helps everyone understand the task.

- *Define process issues to which teacher leaders must conform.* If principals have process preferences, they should share them immediately. Obscuring preferences with words like, "One way I have found that works well is…" implies that what principals are describing is optional. If the approach is not optional due to policies, central office directives, or previous agreed-upon procedures, the principal should make comments like, "I want you to…" or, "A part of what you are to do is…." In turn, when reviewing the project, the conversation should focus on outcomes, not on the processes used, unless there is a lack of progress. Offering someone the opportunity "to run with it" but then criticizing and directing their methods even though they are accomplishing the identified outcome will create a sense of distrust and perhaps even cause the teacher leader to opt out. If it is not illegal, immoral, or unethical, teacher leaders should be encouraged to do it their way, as long as there is progress toward the outcome.

- *Create completion timelines and "big picture maps" for viewing multiple projects simultaneously.* A multitude of activities occur simultaneously in schools. While there may be a sequence for each, the actual operations of the school are not linear. "Big picture" maps with timelines that clearly identify both routine and special events will help minimize redundancies and overlaps and keep everyone informed. Everyone is busy enough without doing jobs that someone else has already done. Helping teachers identify how their work coordinates with others is essential.

- *Provide resources for accomplishing the tasks.* Once the task to be accomplished and the process to be used are agreed upon, conversations turn to what resources are needed. No one can be expected to work without resources such as money, support staff services, time, or physical space. Additionally, teacher leaders should know how to request resources and principals should inform support staff about who is empowered to request services. If there are budget limits, teacher leaders need to know them before their work begins. It is better to cancel or modify the project than to create disappointment and distrust through inadequate resource allocations.

Another resource often overlooked is information. Teacher leaders need access to information relevant to the tasks in which they are involved. Information is gathered in schools for a variety of purposes, particularly reports for the school system, state, and federal entities. Also, principals have access to information that can help teacher leaders when they share information connected to their work.

Finally, time for people to work together is an essential resource for getting things accomplished. Ways to connect can include face-to-face opportunities, conference calls, and electronic exchanges. A few meetings before and after school are understandable; however, locating time during the workday is essential to demonstrate to teacher leaders the priority their efforts take.

■ *Create continuous feedback loops for evaluation and planning.* Principals take on the roles of mentor *and* evaluator. Principals can delegate work, but they cannot abdicate responsibility for the work. They can, however, keep themselves apprised of a project's progress through a monitoring system established to provide teacher leaders the opportunity to share how things are going, get feedback on their work, and have a skilled coach to help them improve. Monitoring can be defined as "focusing on [paying attention to] a project, process, or program by gathering information that (a) indicates whether or not expectations are being achieved, and (b) if not, provides relevant data for designing needed adjustments or corrective actions, which will result in the achievement of expectations" (Pankake, 1998, p. 108).

> **From the Field** The critical thing that I do to ensure the academic success of children at this school is that I monitor it.
>
> *Debbie Backus*
> Former Principal, Montview Elementary School Aurora, Colorado (McREL, 2000)

Structures to Facilitate the Distribution of Power and Authority

Accomplishing a shared vision for student learning requires structures to support the work of teachers. "If the structure is overlooked, an organization often misdirects energy and resources" (Bolman & Deal, 2003, p. 67). These structures are focused on decision making and professional learning.

The structures will vary depending on the school context, but there is one aspect that is nonnegotiable: collaboration. Structures should be designed so that all teachers' voices can be heard. Of course, there will be teachers who, even with these structures in place, will remain silent, but if principals design and communicate the purpose of these options, other teachers can gently pressure the reticent to bring their concerns forward. For too long, relying on teacher volunteerism to collaborate has resulted in pockets of excellence rather than improvement for all students. Collaboration must be an expectation embedded in the culture rather than an invitation or a suggestion (DuFour, 2003). Principals and teacher leaders can establish structures with guidelines for participation and intentionally support teachers to ensure that they work together to focus on student achievement.

See Tool 5.5 Page 124.

All schools have existing structures, but as principals look to promote teacher leadership, a few structures may need to be created, redesigned, or even eliminated. There are structures that are ongoing and focus on governance issues, and others that are specialized and may be continuous or formed on an as-needed basis. In either case, the important point is that once the teams are formed and their task has been made clear, they are empowered to move forward with autonomy and authority to accomplish the task. Listed below are examples of structures that could be intentionally designed to build teacher leadership:

- *Leadership teams.* Leadership teams include members representing different factions of the school community. The members make collective decisions regarding strategic schoolwide decisions. Many states mandate this decision-making structure; policies may dictate what groups will be represented (for example, parents, teachers, or students). Sometimes called shared decision-making or school improvement teams, leadership teams can be critical structures in authentically facilitating the distribution of power and authority. Initially, the principal may be directive in organizing the team, but in time, procedures to ensure that the team has a composition that allows for multiple perspectives and a rotating membership that brings in new people on a regular basis should be in place.

- *Professional development committee.* This group is responsible for making decisions in collaboration with the leadership team regarding the use of limited resources for professional learning. These two groups must work together closely. In too many schools, the professional development committee allocates resources based on teacher seniority and other criteria that are unrelated to the school's vision for student learning. When this committee is effective, members of the group track down internal and external resources to support professional learning. This includes writing grants, visiting other schools, attending external professional development to evaluate its value, and performing other tasks that help them make wise decisions about professional learning.

- *Communication structures.* Information is power. If teachers lack information, their power to lead is diminished. Often principals and other leaders have information that they want to share with teachers, but the busy demands of the school day prevent this information from being distributed. While this is usually unintentional, the results are the same as if the principal chose to keep the information secret. To avoid this, structures must be built to ensure that critical information is shared with everyone. These structures might include electronic mail, weekly staff newsletters, or even a large dry erase board near the teachers' mailboxes.

> **From the Field** We get a Friday "memo" from the principal in our box at the end of each week. Not only does it include all the managerial stuff so we don't have to have faculty meetings—we have NO faculty meetings off the clock.
>
> *Dayle Timmons,* NBCT
> Special Education Teacher,
> TLN Member
> 2004 Florida Teacher of the Year

Communication "trees" can be established through which the principal shares information with one person and that person then shares with other teacher leaders who, in turn, share with all the teachers. Additionally, minutes from meetings should be made public so that everyone has access to a record of these discussions.

- *Teaching teams.* Teaching teams, whether grade-level or subject-centered, support the core of collaboration; it is within these groups that teachers who share common students work together to focus on student learning. Teacher leaders are the key to the success of these teams. Teacher leaders can help ensure that scheduled time is used to make decisions about teaching and learning, rather than individual projects or operational tasks.

- *Faculty study groups.* Study groups provide an opportunity to transform even traditional faculty meetings from a tedious obligation to an anticipated opportunity, if the principal is willing to use these meetings for activities other than information dissemination. Depending on the size of the faculty and the focus of the school change, the structure of these groups will vary, but they should allow for all faculty members to have input into how the change will emerge. Most often, teachers can lead these meetings, either jointly with the principal or alone.

- *Curriculum teams.* Curriculum teams frequently are developed to design and implement the strategic plan that focuses on the vision for student learning. These teams make decisions regarding teaching and learning, such as selecting materials, analyzing student learning data, determining the curriculum scope and sequence, and evaluating the curriculum. Teachers with specialized knowledge of subject matter or curriculum development are required for this work.

- *Management teams.* Management teams are organized to handle the day-to-day issues facing every school. Too often, leadership teams get bogged down in the minutiae of issues such as student extracurricular activities, teacher duties, or access to supplies. Having another team may appear to be inefficient, but separating discussions on these topics keeps the leadership team focused on student learning.

For example, schedule development is an activity that affects students, teachers, parents, cafeteria workers, custodians, office staff, and administrators. Schedules also play a significant role in the instructional process. There are a variety of factors in schedules, such as classes (required and elective), recesses and study halls, computer labs, lunch periods, assemblies, special instructional programs, and others as the situation demands. Schedule development could be an administrative task or it could be a task for a management team.

- *Procedures for hiring new staff.* Selecting and hiring teachers are among the most crucial decisions in any school. The selection of new teachers should take into consideration how they will add value to this new way of leading and learning. Establishing small groups or teams of teachers to participate in the selection process is an empowering activity.

> **From the Field** What I thought was interesting was that the principals, many of which lack the knowledge to understand the safety issues involved with teaching science or other curriculum areas, are asked to choose [new teachers] from a population of people who lack essential skills in the classroom, such as lab safety and student lab safety.
>
> Anonymous by request

Principals will need to work with teacher leaders to determine whether the group will play an advisory role or make the final decisions and provide professional development on interviewing techniques, legal and illegal questions, note taking, and ways to judge interviewees' responses.

- *Induction program for new teachers.* The induction of new teachers cannot be left to chance; new teachers have the potential to contribute to the school's human and social capital. These teachers must understand the culture in which they will be working and the expectations for them to lead and learn. Rather than a hit-or-miss approach, there must be a structure in place to work with teachers new to the school. The induction may supply anything from basic information to intensive support for classroom activities. Some teachers may want to work with beginning teachers, while other teachers will prefer to mentor veteran teachers; there will also be teachers who may want to help but do not want to be consistently involved. This is an area where one teacher leader can assume the power and authority to organize and manage the overall process while keeping the principal informed.

- *Social events and activities.* In most schools, there are planned social events and activities. The purposes of the events vary, but timely planning and careful organization are necessary if the intended purposes are to be achieved. A committee or task force for scheduling and organizing social events and activities is another structure for distributing power and authority. While everyone generally enjoys participating in these events, not everyone likes the planning and organizing. However, in most schools there are those individuals who could probably have second careers as events managers on cruise ships. Building on the interests and skills of these individuals is a way to address important rituals in the organization.

These are only a few examples of the types of structures that can be designed to involve teachers and support their leadership. Structures should be revisited periodically to see if they are fulfilling a need or simply existing because they have always been a part of the school. The members of the organizational structures should have clarity about their roles and responsibilities, which include the following:

- Developing procedures for selecting and rotating representatives so that all members of the school community are represented

- Establishing clear delineation of parameters for making decisions

- Setting up communication and dissemination mechanisms so information is available to everyone in the school community

- Organizing meeting schedules that prevent conflict for teacher leaders who participate in more than one structure.

Summary

Agreeing to distribute power and authority is one of the most difficult decisions a principal will make, because although the school may reap benefits, there will be obstacles. Yet with demands for increased accountability for student learning, principals who want to succeed cannot continue to "go it alone." Instead, they must reach out to teachers for expanded leadership throughout the school. Once the decision is made to distribute power and authority, the principal's work has just begun. Specific actions must take place to build a shared vision, collaborate in decision making, and delegate effectively. These actions take place within purposeful structures designed to promote, build, and sustain teacher leading and learning.

Principals can use the Distributing Power and Authority Rubric (Figure 5.2) to self-assess beliefs about distributing power and authority. The primary goal for building relationships and distributing power and authority is to promote continuous teacher and student learning. Teacher leadership emerges from teachers who are learners. The principal's responsibility is to ensure that quality professional learning is accessible for teachers.

Figure 5.2. Distributing Power and Authority Rubric

Quality teacher leadership requires authentic distribution of power and authority.	
Unsure & Unskilled	Principal does not trust teachers to lead and be accountable. May have one or two individuals with whom issues are discussed and some projects delegated, but only with close supervision.
Moving Along	Principal is beginning to trust a select group of teacher leaders to lead and be accountable. The teacher leaders are generally those individuals in formal leadership roles in the school.
Leading Teacher Leaders	Principal has confidence that most teachers will lead and be accountable

Resources

5.1 Lambert, L. (2003). *Leadership capacity for lasting school improvement*. Alexandria, VA: Association for Supervision and Curriculum Development—Lambert provides 11 specific strategies principals can use to "break dependency relationships" (pp. 48–49).

5.2 Calabrese, R. L., Short, G., & Zepeda, S. J. (1996). *Hands-on leadership tools for principals*. Larchmont, NY: Eye on Education—The authors provide a "step-by-step approach to developing a vision" (pp. 70–89).

5.3 Pace Productivity. (n.d.). How to Delegate website—Provides a brief overview of excuses for not delegating, what to delegate, and delegation instructions. Retrieved on September 25, 2005, from http://www.getmoredone.com/tips9.html

Tools

Tool 5.1   A Guided Reflection: Remembering My Teacher Leader Experiences

To prepare for this activity, take time to find documents that will help in this guided reflection. As you examine the evidence, you will be astounded at how many times you took on leadership roles which you may not have seen as "leadership" at the time.

Step 1: To remember your teacher leader experiences, look for documents reflecting your tenure as a classroom teacher, such as the following:

- Résumé that lists all professional teaching experiences
- Certificates, plaques, and other items that reflect the appreciation of others
- Transcripts from universities or records of professional development activities
- Letters of thanks from students, parents, principals, and others
- Brochures, handbooks, and other publications you wrote or helped write
- Curricular documents, handbooks, and other written materials that were the result of committees on which you served or perhaps even led
- Photos of sports, social, and academic activities in which you were involved

- Newspaper clippings, student yearbooks, and other documentation in which your name appeared or which described a project in which you were involved

Step 2: Look through the documents to find examples of when you assumed both formal and informal leadership roles. Use a chart like the one in Figure 5.3 to make chronological notes about the evolution of your leadership. A sample, excerpted from a principal's chart, is provided in Figure 5.4.

Figure 5.3. Chart of Leadership Roles

Year(s)	Location/School	Informal Leadership	Formal Leadership

Figure 5.4. Excerpted Sample from a Completed Chart of Leadership Roles

Year(s)	Location/School	Informal Leadership	Formal Leadership
1–3	Sanders Middle School	Formed a study group for students with reading problems	Coached boys' basketball team
		Learned new reading strategy with another teacher on the team and worked together to use it with our students	
4–8	Middleton Middle School	Developed an interdisciplinary unit that culminated with a field trip across the state	Served as department chair

Step 3: Respond to the statements in the chart in Figure 5.5.

Figure 5.5. Leadership Actions Chart

Yes	No	Leadership Actions
		1. I extended my energy to projects that made a difference in student learning that were beyond my normal teaching responsibilities.
		2. Others joined me in making the project a success.
		3. The principal or other administrators invited me to work on a project.
		4. I agreed to help the administrator because I trusted this individual.
		5. Some teachers were negative about my involvement in a project.
		6. I sought public recognition for my contributions to the project.
		7. In order for the project to be successful, I had to learn new knowledge or skills.
		8. I found time to complete the project.
		9. There were frustrations as I worked with other adults on the project.
		10. There were times when I resented the time the projects took from my personal life.

Step 4: Use a chart like the one in Figure 5.6 to analyze your past teacher leadership experiences. Recall the school culture in which the work occurred. The "health" of that culture helped determine how pervasive teacher leadership was in that school. In the chart, list your teacher leader experiences and categorize them as rewarding or frustrating.

Figure 5.6. Teacher Leadership Experiences Chart

Experience/ Location	1. _____	2. _____	3. _____
Rewarding or Frustrating			
Self			
One Colleague			
Multiple Colleagues			
Students			
Parents			
Community Leaders			
Central Office			
Others			

Step 5: Look over all of the experiences on the chart and determine if the leadership opportunities were self-initiated or started through the encouragement of colleagues, administrators, or other individuals. There may be multiple columns checked depending on the situation. Then review the chart to identify common characteristics of the people who provided options to lead.

Step 6: Answer this question: How do the leadership experiences noted on the chart connect with your current work to promote, build, and sustain teacher leadership?

Tool 5.2   *Creating a Personal Vision Statement*

Purpose

Write your personal vision statement to clarify your own beliefs and values regarding distributing power and authority, trusting teachers, and promoting and supporting teacher leadership.

Definition

A vision statement is a written description of a desired or ideal state regarding your personal and professional roles to be achieved sometime in the future. "In a nutshell, your personal vision is what you want to be, do, feel, think, own, associate with, and impact by some date in the future" (Phillips-Jones, retrieved August 11, 2005, from http://www.mentoring group.com).

Rationale

A personal vision statement "guides us in the decisions we make and the directions we take" (Peterkin, 2003). Creating a personal vision statement helps to focus thoughts and draw the individual in a desired direction. Rushfeldt (retrieved August 11, 2005) adds, "Your vision statement serves as a compass to keep things going in the right direction. It helps you measure your progress, set goals, establish priorities, and know when to use one of the most important words in your vocabulary: No." The activity of actually writing the personal vision statement is essential for increasing the strength of your commitment to achieve it.

Quality Measure

A personal vision statement should be more than just words and a series of sentences, and "it should stir enthusiasm and excitement" (Rushfeldt, retrieved August 11, 2005). The following questions are helpful in assessing the quality and completeness of the statement created:

- Does it represent challenging yet realistic outcomes?
- Is it inspiring and energizing?
- Does it communicate its essential message directly and succinctly?
- Does it provide you with a clear sense of what type of leader you want to become? (Delta Gamma, retrieved on August 11, 2005, from http://www.deltagamma.org/vision_statement.shtml)

Step 1: See a picture in your mind.

1. What would you be doing in a future that reflects sustained teacher leadership and implementation of distributed power and authority?
2. What relationships would be in place that are not there now?
3. How have your roles and responsibilities changed in relationship to the emergence of teacher leaders?
4. What has happened to the way in which decisions are made?
5. What is the state of student learning?
6. Have teacher and principal learning opportunities changed? How? What do they look like in this future state?

Step 2: Capture the dimensions in words. With this mental image as your guide, begin to write down what you see in this future state.

What values are evident in this picture of the future? (Values held by you? By teachers? By students? By district personnel?)

What are the behaviors occurring in this picture of the future that are not occurring now?

What are the results of these behaviors in terms of student and adult learning, organizational culture, and leadership?

Step 3: Pull it together in a word picture. Look carefully at each of the descriptions written in response to the guiding questions in Step 2. Begin to synthesize the information in each of the three questions into a personal vision statement that is limited to 50 to 75 words—no more.

Step 4: Share the word picture turned personal vision statement with a friend or close colleague—someone you trust. Talk with this individual about the statement. Ask them to listen and, if appropriate, ask you questions that will help clarify your thinking. (It is not this person's role to judge whether this vision is one you should pursue, only to help you get clarity.) Based on the information received from your colleague or friend, edit the statement if necessary.

Step 5: Begin moving toward the future you described.

When completed, the vision statement needs to be kept in a place that will provide opportunity for you to see it for inspiration and to use it to devise strategies for making your vision a reality. It is also true that the statement may need to be revised or reaffirmed periodically as the movement toward the future described gets under way.

Resources for Writing a Personal Vision Statement

http://www.deltagamma.org

http://www.eyekai.tv/Articles/writing_your_personal_vision.htm

http://www.ecareersolutions.com/adultintro.html

http://www.lifetoolsforwomen.com/p/write-mission-vision.htm

http://resources.sai-iowa.org/si/desiredfuture/vision.html

Tool 5.3 Decision Making Chart

Test	Criteria	Low	→	→	→	→	→	→	High
		1	2	3	4	5	6	7	8	9
Relevance	Level of interest in decision area									
Expertise	Level of expertise in decision area									
Jurisdiction	Level of authority regarding decision area									
Intensity	Level of desire to be involved									

9	
8	
7	
6	
5	
4	
3	
2	
1	
	Relevance Expertise Jurisdiction Intensity

Once the scores are plotted, you and others will need to determine what the benchmark scores are for each "test." You will also need to determine how many of the "tests" need to have high scores for an individual or group to be included in a decision area. This tool cannot do that for you; it can only help you think through important elements and provide a visual display to start the conversation about the selection process.

Tool 5.4   *Project Delegation Form*

Use the form in Figure 5.8 as a standard discussion and recording tool during conversations regarding the delegation of leadership responsibilities. Every situation is unique; the content and number of questions needed may vary. If each item is thoroughly addressed, both the principal and teacher leader will have a solid understanding of the work to be done. Additionally, this form can be used by teacher leaders as they work with their teacher colleagues on projects.

Figure 5.8. Project Delegation Form

Date: _____

The desired result of this effort is _____
_____.

The targeted date for completion of this effort is _____
_____.

Processes/actions required as a part of this effort are _____
_____.

Parameters that must be observed in carrying out this work are
_____.

Resources available for accomplishing this work include the following:

Personnel	Who?
Space	Where? For what purpose?
Time	When? How arranged?
Funding	Accessed through whom?

Tool 5.5   School Structures Inventory

Directions

1. Identify the current structures in which teachers participate in the inventory chart in Figure 5.9.

2. Indicate the major purpose of the structures.

3. For any of the structures for which you mark "yes," take time to list the names of each individual who is currently working within that structure.

4. Add structures not listed on the chart.

5. Analyze the data:

    a. Are a variety of purposes served through one to two structures or through many?

    b. Does a review of the participants in the current structures indicate that most, if not all, faculty members are involved in at least one of the structures? If not, who is missing? Who is serving within multiple structures?

    c. Do the structures in place advance the school's vision for student learning?

    d. What structures should be added or discontinued?

Figure 5.9. School Structures Inventory

Existing Structures	Yes	No	Major Purpose (For example, collective learning, governance, social)	Current Participants
Leadership Team				
Communication				
Teaching Teams				
Curriculum Teams				
Study Groups				
Management Team				
Faculty Social Committee				
Professional Development Committee				
Induction Program				
Faculty/Staff Hiring Procedures				
Others				

6

Aligning Teacher Leadership with Professional Learning

Quality teacher leadership aligns with professional learning to help achieve the school's shared vision for student learning. The relationships between the two are mutually beneficial because growth in teacher learning supports growth in teacher leadership, and in time, growth in teacher leadership influences teacher learning. National, state, and local school system reforms rely on this partnership of leading and learning, because only with internal leadership can these programs develop and be sustained.

From the Field If the staff development is to be meaningful, time must be devoted to the internalization of it...and we know how much time teachers have. Having it on site helps with this. Professional development is not one size fits all.

Tina Link
Science Teacher, TLN Member
Kennesaw, Georgia

Teachers are flooded with both mandated and voluntary professional learning opportunities, some of which are worthwhile. Unfortunately, most are considered a waste of time by teachers. Sparks (2005), executive director of the National Staff Development Council, shared, "My work in the field of staff development for the past 25 years has revealed to me deep feelings of discontent among countless teachers, administrators, and policymakers regarding the quality of professional learning in schools" (pp. 8–9). Yet most teachers know how they learn new teaching behaviors that affect student learning, as evidenced by the results of a national sample of more than 1,000 teachers. Here is what these teachers wanted in their professional learning:

- Sustained and intensive professional learning over time
- Active learning
- Professional learning that is coherent, connected to what I am doing with my students
- Content focused on what I teach (Garet, Porter, Desimone, Birman, & Yoon, 2001).

In this chapter, we first invite principals to think differently about professional learning for teachers. Then we ask them to conduct a self-study of their own professional learning experiences. Next, we describe some group structures and professional learning designs then offer one comprehensive model that illustrates the teacher leading and learning process. Following this, we recommend strategies for principals to consider in confronting reluctant teacher learners.

Thinking Differently About Professional Learning

See Resources 6.1, 6.2 Page 149.

Engaging diverse students who do not respond to traditional approaches to teaching and ensuring full inclusion for students with special needs are two examples of the complex issues educators face. No longer can professional learning be considered simply instruction in models of delivery, such as workshops, study groups, or action research. Instead, the entire school staff must build on their capacity, that is, professional learning, to develop "the collective ability—dispositions, skills, knowledge, motivation, and re-sources—to act together to bring about positive change" (Fullan, 2005, p. 4). Achieving this "collective ability" requires principals to nurture teachers in the construction of meaning in their work. Professional learning models are tools to be used, but the real learning happens in the cycle of conversations, actions, evaluation, and new actions that is supported through intentional leadership that gently pressures and nurtures teachers. This inquiry process must be organizationally embedded rather than externally imposed to build

> **From the Field** We're in a different teaching climate today. Now we have this research that tells us much more about how children learn, and the most effective processes to use…for them to get it. We haven't always had all of this knowledge…. We have to learn that we can improve…without feeling like we've failed in the past…
>
> *Nancy Grogan*
> Principal, Wellborn Elementary School
> Anniston, Alabama (Norton, 2004)

teachers' knowledge and skills, or increase human capital, within the school's social networks.

An examination of the influence of teachers' adult development on their professional learning helps us to understand the level of change that must take place in order to teach differently. For adults to move to another level of development, they must begin to see a gap between what they believe to be accurate and what they are experiencing. To move across this gap involves transformational learning, which demands that the adult be engaged in honest appraisal, reflection, and taking action. Few of us realize this is happening because we believe that life experiences have helped us to mature, when what we are actually doing is changing our long-held beliefs based on new experience. Similarly, teachers do not change their teaching behaviors because they attend a workshop, read a book, or participate in a study group. They must be involved in a variety of professional learning experiences that invite them to examine the discrepancies between how they are teaching and how they need to teach to reach their goals for students.

The complexity of this level of professional learning exceeds the traditional model used in most schools and school systems. For example, if there is a problem with the writing skills of students, a school system may mandate that all teachers attend workshops on the writing process. Another example occurs when a new leader comes to a school or system enamored with a particular program, then mandates that all teachers learn this program. These deficit models ignore that teacher beliefs and their behaviors based on those beliefs are not that pliable. There will be teachers who comply for fear of punishment or lack of approval from formal leaders, but the majority of teachers will listen, or pretend to listen, and then go back to their classrooms and teach based on their own beliefs about how students learn, even if those beliefs are not producing the desired results. "Habits, values, and attitudes, even dysfunctional ones, are part of one's identity. To change the way people see and do things is to challenge how they define themselves" (Heifetz & Linsky, 2002, p. 27). Regardless of the number of supervisors in a school, use of mandated programs cannot be guaranteed. The structure of schools and the culture of teaching do not permit this level of prescription and inspection.

If mandated deficit approaches do not work, then how do teachers change their teaching strategies to better meet students' needs? Teachers must personally see a gap between what they are doing in their classrooms and their desired goals for students before they will use new instructional strategies. This proposed professional learning demands more intentional leadership than asking the professional learning committee to allocate funds for teachers to go to workshops or conferences. The outcome, though, is worthy of the effort, because not only will teachers learn, they will become leaders.

Self-Study:
Experiences with Professional Learning

Principals can realize the importance of aligning teacher leadership with professional learning by reflecting on their own professional learning experiences. Most everyone, including principals, has experienced a wide range of professional learning opportunities, the quality of which ranges from dreadful to fantastic and includes everything in between. Principals may find it easier to understand the importance of key variables in the quality of professional learning experiences by taking a few moments to reflect on their past learning opportunities; doing this can help principals more effectively use the information presented in this chapter.

Step 1: Recall and Respond—Dreadful Experience

First, principals should recall their most dreadful professional learning experience. Principals should try making the memory as vivid as possible, including remembering such details as when it occurred, who was there, or what the intended learning was, then respond to the following statements:

The most dreadful professional learning opportunity I ever experienced		
Took place in a large group.	Yes	No
Involved activities and interactions with other learners.	Yes	No
Was directly connected to my work.	Yes	No
Was sustained and intensive over time.	Yes	No
Took place away from the job site.	Yes	No
Gave me an opportunity to apply or practice what was being learned.	Yes	No
Was largely content-focused.	Yes	No
Dealt mostly with processing.	Yes	No
Was held outside the school workday.	Yes	No
Resulted in improved student learning.	Yes	No

Step 2: Recall and Respond—Fantastic Experience

Now, principals should think back to their most fantastic professional learning experience. Again, they should try to bring to mind as many details as possible about why this was such a fantastic experience and respond to the same set of statements:

The most fantastic professional learning opportunity I ever experienced		
Took place in a large group.	Yes	No
Involved activities and interactions with other learners.	Yes	No
Was directly connected to my work.	Yes	No
Was sustained and intensive over time.	Yes	No
Took place away from the job site.	Yes	No
Gave me an opportunity to apply or practice what was being learned.	Yes	No
Was largely content-focused.	Yes	No
Dealt mostly with processing.	Yes	No
Was held outside the school workday.	Yes	No
Resulted in improved student learning.	Yes	No

Step 3: Compare

A comparison of the two experiences usually reveals that some components are always present in the fantastic experiences and always absent in the dreadful experiences. For example, the size of the group and where the learning opportunity occurred make less difference than the relevance to the principal's work, the opportunity to apply the learning immediately, interaction with others, and follow-up.

We suggest that principals use this same activity with the entire faculty and then follow these next steps:

- Invite faculty members to compare their results within small groups.
- Chart the results. Taking time to list the questions and tally the number of yes and no responses for the fantastic experiences and the dreadful experiences will provide a powerful graphic representation regarding what is really important in planning and provid-

ing quality professional learning opportunities. The charted information can be used to formulate a set of guidelines for planning and evaluating professional learning opportunities for all groups.

 Once the guidelines are established, both the principal and the teachers should examine the existing professional learning and level of support. Any discrepancies between the principal's and the teachers' perceptions should be explored together.

See
Tool 6.1
Page 151.

Structures for Professional Learning

Professional learning can occur through a variety of structures designed for individuals, small groups or teams, or the whole school. Developing and maintaining support of these structures can be daunting, and sometimes a principal needs a "map" to keep track, but as teacher leaders become a part of this design, the system can eventually become self-managing.

Individual Professional Learning

Many teachers take the initiative to learn without direction from anyone by searching for quality professional learning both inside and outside the school or district. The proliferation of websites that attract teachers indicates that they are going to learn in spite of the formal system in place for their professional learning. The certification process through the National Board of Professional Teaching Standards is an example of how teachers work individually to document and reflect on their teaching. Although this process was designed to document accomplished teaching practices rather than as a professional development activity, teachers learn reflection skills that continue beyond the certification process.

External networks attract teachers who can learn from other teacher leaders from diverse settings. Teachers often seek learning in content-area professional associations and then go on to provide leadership in these organizations. Graduate schools offer teachers a higher level of licensure, usually with the incentive of a pay increase; during their study, teachers can find quality learning that is missing in their workplace. These are only a few examples of how teachers can and do take responsibility for their own individual learning.

The principal's role in nurturing individual professional learning is as "matchmaker" between the information they have about professional learning opportunities and teachers' interests and passions. When a teacher is invited to attend a professional learning experience related to what he or she wants to learn, there is potential for adding to the human and social capital of the school as well as for increasing the positive relationship between the principal and the teacher. As follow-up, principals should spend time visiting with teachers to inquire about their application of the learning, identify any additional resources needed, and provide recognition for these professionals. This attention to individual needs results in benefits that far outweigh the investment.

Small Group/Team/Partner Professional Learning

See Resources 6.3, 6.4, 6.5 Page 149.

Within small groups or teams, social networks contribute to increasing human capital, such as teachers' knowledge and skills. These groupings may be voluntary, selected, or based on roles and responsibilities. As classrooms become more and more diverse and challenging in their composition, teachers will need increased peer support. Here are examples of different types of groupings:

- Single subject area
- Focus groups
- Grade level or department teams
- Study groups
- Groups with representatives from each grade, subject, or specialty
- Pairs of teachers in mentoring relationships

The initial sharing may be limited, but it can be an incentive to move to deeper levels of collaborative learning. For example, the sequence for building collaborative groups from less risk to more risk may include the following:

Low Risk

1. Forming study groups around a common topic
2. Offering professional development workshops delivered by teacher leaders
3. Looking at student work and discussing it
4. Inquiring about teaching through action research, portfolios, or video cases
5. Providing time for peer observations of the "expert" teacher with no feedback
6. Conducting joint planning with peer observations and feedback

High Risk

As groups work on their professional learning, the principal's role becomes one of attending to the process. We acknowledge that the principal cannot take part in every learning experience, yet it is important for principals to keep their fingers on the pulse of the activities. They can do this by visiting groups on a regular schedule, talking to key members of the groups, or requesting a debriefing meeting to update them on the status of the learning. Principals also have the responsibility to set expectations that learning groups meet on a regular basis and use the time wisely, as well as monitor the groups to make sure that the expectations are met.

Whole-Faculty Focus

At first, principals take the responsibility for whole-school focus because, in their positions, they are able to see a broader perspective and they have the resources to support these activities. Senge and colleagues (2000) describe this role for the principal as "'lead teacher and lead learner,' and steward of the learning process as a whole" (p. 15). In time, principals can step back as teacher leaders move beyond leadership in their classrooms or in small groups to working with the entire faculty. Again, as with individual and small-group professional learning, the success of these efforts depends on the principal's willingness to be closely involved and supportive with available resources.

Professional Learning Design

See Resources 6.6, 6.7, 6.8 Page 149.

Sometimes the design of professional learning is hastily put together because of the time pressures placed on the leaders responsible for a workshop, event, or activity. Unfortunately, this can result in wasted resources and, most likely, limited or no transfer of knowledge and skills to the classroom. Rather than asking teachers to participate in these activities, principals can seek permission from central office leaders to develop school-site experiences that match the criteria for quality professional learning. This would not prevent individual teachers from attending external professional learning opportunities appropriate for their work, but the majority of the professional learning would take place at the

From the Field At my school, we have endless paid professional development opportunities. However, administration's attitude seems to be, "Well you had a workshop on X, so now it's time to implement it and master it." No further discussion, no ongoing training, nada.

Ellen Berg
Eighth Grade Language Arts and Social Studies, TLN Member
San Diego Cooperative Charter School
San Diego, California

school site. The following elements are essential for quality on-site professional learning programs:

- Analysis of student learning needs to determine the focus of the professional learning
- Involvement of teachers in decision making regarding their own learning
- Design of evaluation of the professional learning before the design is implemented
- Use of research-based strategies for improved instruction
- Placement of responsibility on teacher learners to become "experts" in the instructional strategies so that they can help other teachers learn
- Encouragement of teacher learners to become teacher leaders by demonstrating their new skills
- Scheduling of collaborative support groups for teacher inquiry into their practice
- Evaluation of the student learning outcomes as a result of the teacher learning

We find that principals are somewhat surprised at the level of support needed for teachers to transfer their learning to the classroom. Joyce and Showers (2002), using their research and experience in professional development, predicted the percentage of participants who would actually transfer instructional skills from a professional learning activity, such as a workshop, to the classroom. The table in Figure 6.1 demonstrates how a teacher would have to learn the theory, watch a demonstration, practice the skill, and finally and most important, engage in peer coaching at the school to ensure the skill is used in the classroom. Today, few professional learning activities designed to improve teaching include all four components.

We find that principals are surprised at the level of support needed for teachers to transfer their professional learning to the classroom. A workshop alone is not sufficient. The research of Joyce and Showers (2002) demonstrates the percentage of teachers who actually transfer an instructional strategy from a workshop to skillfully using the strategy in their classrooms. This transfer depends on the teachers' participation in four components: 1) learning the theory supporting the instructional strategy; 2) watching a skillful demonstration of the instructional strategy; 3) practicing the strategy; and 4) finally, and most important, engaging in peer coaching at the school site to ensure the strategy is competently used in the classroom. If a group of teachers experiences only the first three components, as few as five percent (5%) of the teachers transfer and master the strategy in their classrooms (p. 78). If these same teachers participate additionally in substantive follow-up at the school site, such as the peer coaching, it is predicted that 95% of the teachers will transfer the professional learning to the classroom. Today, few professional learning activities designed to improve teaching address all four components, especially follow-up.

It is difficult to condone offering an isolated workshop that does not fit into the context of the school's professional learning goals or does not engage participants in the study of theory, demonstrations, skill practice, and follow-up with peer coaching. There has been substantial research over the last 20 years arguing for designing professional learning based on these conditions. This professional knowledge has been ignored for too long.

See Resources 6.9, 6.10 Page 150.

There are times when a presentation or workshop is the best tool to use. For example, if a new computer software program is purchased by a school and all teachers must use it, then it would not be appropriate to use an inquiry method to learn about the program. Also, the school may have a reason to invite an inspirational speaker for a session to set the tone either before or after a challenging experience for the faculty. If professional learning is well thought out, there should be flexibility that acknowledges alternative approaches to professional learning other than the workshop model. Principals working with central office administrators can gain approval for recertification or licensure credits for unique types of professional learning. Figure 6.1 gives a more comprehensive list of professional learning models that are not "workshops."

Figure 6.1. Options for Professional Learning

If Not a Workshop, Then What?	
• Participating in a study or support group • Doing a classroom walk-through • Giving presentations at conferences • Researching on the Internet • Leading a schoolwide committee or project • Developing displays, bulletin boards • Shadowing students • Coaching a colleague • Being a mentor—being mentored • Joining a professional network • Using a tuning protocol to examine student work • Attending an in-depth institute in a content area • Writing an article about your work	• Analyzing the expectations of your statewide assessments • Enrolling in a university course • Viewing educational videos • Maintaining a professional portfolio • Studying content standards for your state • Observing other teachers teach • Listening to video/audio recordings • Participating in a videoconference or conference calls with experts • Visiting model schools/programs • Developing curriculum • Doing school improvement planning
• Observing model lessons • Reading journals, educational magazines, books • Participating in a critical friends group • Doing a self-assessment • Shadowing another teacher or professional in the field • Keeping a reflective log or journal	• Examining new technological resources to supplement lessons • Being observed and receiving feedback from another teacher or principal • Engaging in lesson study • Working on a strategic planning team

Used by permission from the National Staff Development Council, http://www.nsdc.org

See
Tool 6.2
Page 153.

Good judgment by school leaders is needed to determine what type of professional learning is appropriate, but each decision must be based on the school's shared vision for student learning and available student data. The following discussion identifies the major components necessary to create professional learning communities.

Collective Learning

See
Resource 6.11
Page 150.

Many principals envision their schools as schoolwide professional learning communities where everyone is involved in learning to improve student performance. Making this a reality can be stressful for principals. There are limited examples where a school has been able to maintain the focus on professional learning. When schools are identified as professional learning communities, the strong leadership of a principal is always a primary factor, but sustaining the professional learning community after the principal leaves can be difficult. As more emphasis is placed on building teacher leadership, the possibility that school change can be sustained increases.

Forming collaborative learning teams is at the heart of professional learning communities. We recommend a framework adapted from Joyce and Showers (2002) using four components that principals and teacher leaders can design to ensure needed support for collaboration.

Component 1: Time and Space

Quality time and space for the collaboration is a prerequisite. Asking teachers to find their own time and space is unrealistic and sends a message that collaboration is not important. The National Staff Development Council recommends that 25 percent of a teacher's contract time be spent on professional learning (Killion, 2002). Most schools are a long way from meeting this goal, but targeting this percentage of time indicates that professional learning should not be grabbed in spare minutes within planning periods or beyond the contract day. Principals can use structures such as teaching schedules, substitute teacher teams, and room assignments to facilitate finding time and space to support collaboration.

Component 2: Start Early

If teachers are going to learn together, their collaboration should begin as soon as they start working on a common program. In the comprehensive model we share later in this chapter, these groups may form after a few teachers have gained the knowledge and skills to use a specific teaching strategy or with all teachers immediately. The decision on how and when groups form should be made in context, but principals can be alert to providing different levels of support depending on where members of the team are in their personal contexts.

Component 3: Provide Guidelines

Guidelines help teachers learn how to collaborate with each other. Too many well-meaning efforts by principals result in teachers coming together without knowing what they are supposed to do. Generating substantive conversations about teaching and learning demands skills many teachers do not have. Additionally, they may have worked autonomously for so long that they may be unwilling to share or may actually fear that other teachers will find out that they do not know all the answers.

Component 4: Accountability

Professional learning, whether alone or in groups, demands accountability. If principals are providing resources and teachers are spending valuable time working together, there should be a difference in the students' learning. Establishing and using measures to link professional learning to student success is a strategy that persuades teachers to continue their work together.

A Comprehensive Professional Leading and Learning Model

There is extensive literature on what quality professional learning is, but there are few concrete models that give principals specific steps to follow to establish the level of professional learning we are describing in this book. There are other models that may be appropriate depending on the teaching culture; however, we present this one model to demonstrate how teacher leadership and teacher learning can be aligned.

Where professional learning starts is unpredictable, because it depends on the human and social resources and the school's culture for professional learning. In most schools, an invitation to learn is offered and only a few teachers accept; this, then, is where the professional learning community begins. There is a "ripple effect" that can move the learning beyond the group to reach most of the faculty. In every school there will be teachers who never join this learning community, and principals will need to confront these reluctant learners. In other cases, some teachers will look for positions in other schools, where they will not be expected to be a part of the professional learning community.

The work in this comprehensive model begins with small groups of teachers and then expands over time to include all teachers; it includes five phases: gap analysis, development of a vision for desired outcomes, involvement of professionals in readiness experiences and decision making, formation of a professional learning evaluation plan, and entry of the professional learning community in a continuous "learning and leading cycle." This cycle is based on strategies used by an exceptional middle school principal that resulted in sustained teacher leading and learning (Gonzales, 2004).

Phase 1: Gap Analysis

Today, learning for all students is not an option, it is an expectation. We have a moral obligation to provide quality education so that all students can learn. This requires an examination of what level of student performance exists and comparing that to what we want students to achieve. The gap analysis should be the driving force for decisions about quality professional learning. Without this information about student learning, it is impossible to effectively determine the learning needs of teachers.

Phase 2: Vision Development

From the data obtained in the gap analysis, the faculty and staff determine a vision and action plan. The vision influences where the investment of resources, both human and fiscal, should be made in professional learning in order to meet the expectation of learning for all students. Teachers are invited to contribute to planning the professional learning, but principals ensure that plans are based on student data rather than on a generic survey of teacher-perceived needs. Professional learning should add value to the school's human and social capital, reflect the teachers' individual differences, and still remain focused on the vision.

Phase 3: Readiness

After a vision for student performance is established, the principal and teachers search for strategies to address the gap in student performance. There are countless ways this readiness phase could play out. The purpose is to find research-based information and best-practice strategies that address the students' learning needs. Listed below are a few suggestions to help principals and teachers jump-start the process:

- Form a task group to examine books, journal articles, and websites addressing the identified needs.
- Attend professional conferences and select relevant concurrent sessions.
- Visit schools with similar demographics where there is exemplary student performance in the area of concern.

- Search out and communicate with national networks where teacher leaders and others are focused on the issue or issues the analysis has defined.

It is best not to spend too much time in this readiness phase. Decisions must be made to move quickly into action. Fullan (1993) suggests that we spend too much time on planning before getting into the work; rather than using the process of "ready, aim, fire," we should consider using "ready, fire, aim" (p. 31), because moving into action allows us an opportunity to refine the plan while working on it.

Phase 4: Evaluation Process

Whether the investment in professional learning is worthwhile is measured in terms of student learning and performance. Before beginning professional learning, specific, measurable student learning goals must be established and a plan developed to determine how to evaluate the process used to meet these goals. There is a tendency to rely too heavily on test data for evaluation, so the evaluation plan should include other authentic assessment methods that help determine needed adjustments to the plan.

Phase 5: Learning and Leading

This constructivist phase exemplifies the use of existing resources in order to build human and social capital. If principals understand how to build positive relationships, as discussed in Chapter 4, this phase requires putting that information into action to create social networks in which teachers develop knowledge, beliefs, and skills for improved instruction. To promote a learning community that results in organizational learning, it is important to recognize that learning is a social enterprise. In order to transform teacher behaviors, professional learning must connect teachers' emotions and their intellect. The steps in the cycle below tap into knowledge, skills, and emotions through the "shared network of social situations" (Gonzales, 2004, p. 45). Figure 6.2 illustrates how teacher learning results in teacher leadership, which then can spread throughout the school.

Figure 6.2. Teacher Learning Results in Teacher Leadership

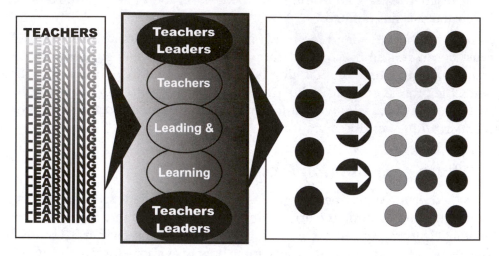

Step 1: Invitation

Invite teachers to participate in a study group focused on a selected teaching strategy from Phase 3. Extend the invitation to all teachers. Of course, not all teachers will come, but the teachers who accept the invitation become the core group. At first, the principal is the person who secures materials for the study group, but as teacher leadership emerges, this responsibility will move off the principal's plate.

Step 2: Learning the Strategy

Send at least two teachers out to learn the teaching strategy. There are a variety of ways teachers can learn instructional strategies, such as attending a workshop, visiting a school to observe the strategies in action, or joining an external network of teacher leaders who have struggled with the same issue and are willing to share. It is important to send at least two teachers so that when the teachers return they can reinforce each other in the learning process. Regardless of the source of the learning, in the beginning, principals should go with the teachers and be colearners. As this model is sustained, teacher leaders take the place of the principal as the support system for other teachers sent out to find solutions to student learning problems.

Step 3: Reassembling and Providing Support

When the teachers from Step 2 return from learning, too often they are left on their own. Even before they leave to learn, a system should be in place to bring the study group from Step 1 back together to support the teachers as they begin using the new skills. Other teachers are not obliged to use the new skills, but they and the principal should nurture the teacher learners as they face the inevitable disappointments involved in using a new skill in the classroom.

Step 4: Implementation

In too many schools, teachers are asked to attend a workshop to learn a skill and then come back to teach other teachers. While this appears to be a good use of resources, it does not work well in most cases. Teachers cannot teach a skill that they have not used. Teachers must use and refine the skills in their own classrooms before they can help other teachers learn the skills.

Step 5: Continued Support

Continue support group meetings for the teacher learners. Membership in this support group may vary, but if the principal and a few interested teachers join with the teacher learners to reflect on their experiences, it will reinforce the importance of their work. This ongoing, nurturing support is vital to the success of professional learning, especially at the beginning.

Step 6: Demonstration

Invite other teachers to observe teacher learners demonstrating the new teaching strategy. Once the teacher learners are comfortable with the new strategy, it is time to extend an invitation to all teachers to learn. The teacher leaders may offer a workshop or open their classrooms for teacher observation. The teacher learners now become the teacher leaders.

Step 7: Coaching

Ask teacher leaders to coach other teachers who are willing to try the new teaching strategy by modeling the teaching strategy. Teachers may invite a teacher leader to come into their classrooms while they experiment with the strategy. They may work together as team teachers, or the teacher leader can observe and provide feedback.

Step 8: Ongoing Support

To sustain the momentum in using new teaching strategies, teacher learners need to come together to share what is happening in their classrooms and seek out feedback in order to make adjustments. The teacher leaders can serve as facilitators of the discussions, offer assistance through coaching, and identify needed resources. Principals continue to maintain a connection to these groups so that they can provide resources and reinforce continuous learning.

Step 9: Evaluation

Evaluate the process and student performance. The evaluation plan developed during Phase 3 is used to collect data throughout the process for both making adjustments and providing measures for a final determination regarding the achievement of student learning goals. This does not have to be a complicated process, but it is important to measure the success of the professional learning in terms of student outcomes.

Reluctant Teacher Learners

See
Tool 6.3
Page 154.

Predictably, there will be teachers, especially at first, who will not be willing to participate in professional learning regardless of the incentives. These teachers are reluctant for a variety of reasons, including the personal context issues discussed in Chapter 3. Often the most resistant teachers are those who in the past were strong advocates for innovations but became disillusioned. Then there are teachers who cherish their autonomy and feel that involvement in collaborative professional learning will reduce their independence and impinge on their time for working with students. Finally, there are teachers who are mediocre or incompetent, yet they may not see themselves in this way.

Disillusioned Teachers

Many teachers become enthusiastic about professional learning and spend their valuable time learning and working to make a program succeed with their students. After the teachers are involved, the principal or the central office leaders stop the support of the program and jump to a new initiative. After facing multiple new programs and their accompanying professional development, usually within a short time frame, teachers experience overload, and their enthusiasm is replaced with skepticism.

Principals should acknowledge that these teachers' history with change may have been unpleasant. Conversations with disillusioned teachers about what has happened in the past can reveal patterns of manipulation, inadequate resources, and disrespect for the professionalism of these teachers. It may be necessary for the faculty and staff to revisit past experiences, recognize the misuse of professional learning, and establish norms for how initiatives and professional learning will take place in the future. Making the past public gives the disillusioned teachers affirmation that their experiences were unfortunate, but in the future they will be supported and expected to be learners.

Teacher Individuality

There are teachers who select the teaching profession because they do not have to work closely with other adults and can focus their energy on students. For whatever reasons, these individuals believe that they can succeed by securing their own resources, inventing teaching strategies, and developing relationships with their students. Although most of these teachers are social in public areas of the school, they retreat to their classrooms as soon as they can to protect their time and space. In a traditional school, these teachers may give up on the more challenging students (Talbert & McLaughlin, 2002), but a school with a vision of learning for all students cannot permit this to happen.

The principal must "emphasize what is meant by autonomy. Emphasize freedom to, not freedom from" (Blasé & Kirby, 1992, p. 61). The principal can use social networks to build authentic collaboration while still respecting teachers' individuality. This will allow teachers to see the benefit of collaboration for the students they are not able to reach, yet still maintain some individuality and autonomy.

Teachers of Concern

There are teachers who do not see professional learning as part of their job responsibilities. These are the teachers who fulfill the minimum renewal requirements for licensure or participate in professional learning without being an active learner. Some of these teachers are not lacking ability, but they are mediocre. Other teachers are incompetent, but not to the point that a principal can document and recommend their dismissal.

Mediocre Teachers

Mediocre teachers usually do not see or admit that they have problems in their teaching. If problems are pointed out to them, they usually do not believe it is their problem, and they blame negative results with their students on the students' backgrounds or lack of parent support. Parent complaints, poor student performance, and discipline problems are but a few of the outcomes resulting from the mediocre teacher's performance, and each demands an inordinate amount of attention from administrators. Principals should resist the temptation to avoid contact with these teachers in the hopes that they will improve their teaching on their own. It will not happen.

In the traditional performance appraisal process, principals are faced with an overload of teacher evaluations. Mediocre teachers may have previous positive evaluations on file; thus, it is difficult to move them toward improved performance. Unfortunately, principals tend to identify professional learning, such as attending a workshop, observing another teacher, or reading an article, as an improvement goal. There are two reasons this approach is not effective. First, the performance problems may not be learning problems; instead, they may be based on something else, such as the teacher's personal situation or a long-held belief that teaching is a job fulfilled only to provide resources for participation in activities outside the school. Second, if the performance problems are skill related, sending a teacher out alone to learn will rarely change teaching behaviors. Teachers may comply with the principal's mandate to participate in a professional learning experience, but their beliefs and teaching strategies will remain unchanged.

An alternative approach to working with mediocre teachers is to refrain from focusing on their deficits. To do this, leaders can build structures in which mediocre teachers work with other teachers to be accountable for student learning. Another strategy for this is a 12-step approach to connecting supervision and evaluation (Marshall, 2005). In this model, Marshall moves the focus from the individual teacher to teams of teachers who are accountable for common lesson planning, assessments, and results. The final individual evaluation of teachers is based on a scoring guide similar to the rubrics teachers develop for assessing student work.

See
Resource 6.12
Page 150.

Most states and school systems have performance appraisal systems in place to evaluate teachers. These systems range from the once-a-year visit by the principal or another administrator to comprehensive clinical supervision models. In all these models, the legal responsibility for making judgments regarding teacher performance rests with the principal. There are efforts to improve the traditional teacher evaluation process, which most teachers know does not help them improve their teaching. Four trends to change the traditional teacher evaluation model may impact teacher mediocrity in the future:

- *Peer assistance.* This process taps into competent teachers to help mediocre teachers. In many school systems, the peer assistance program is developed in collaboration with the teachers' union.
- *The standards movement.* The standards and their accompanying accountability put pressure on mediocre teachers to perform.

- *Teacher portfolios.* Teachers must present evidence of their performance over time in a portfolio.
- *Data about student performance.* The focus here is not on what the teacher is doing, but how the students are learning. Although high-stakes tests are often the source of these data, there are other authentic strategies to collect such data. (Adapted from Platt, Tripp, Ogden, & Fraser, 2000, pp. 181–191.)

Principals are obligated to work within the existing teacher evaluation process in their school systems, but they can move toward building alternate structures in which teachers are responsible for the learning of all students, not just those students in their individual classrooms. Then professional learning decisions to improve performance are based on student needs rather than a quick fix to make the mediocre teacher better.

Incompetent Teachers

With mediocre teachers, there is at least hope that with pressure and resources, they can improve their teaching. Incompetent teachers are those who may exist in a deep phase of withdrawal, who simply show up to work but not teach, or who are emotionally unstable to the point that students are at risk in their classrooms. We might tolerate a mediocre teacher, but the incompetent teachers are the ones we would never allow to teach our own children. Principals know who these teachers are, dread the complicated process to remove them from the profession, and may shrink from addressing the problem. Helping these teachers goes way beyond professional learning, demanding a level of support that is not available in most school systems. When students are in danger, either intellectually, physically, or emotionally, intentional leaders have no choice but to put in the energy and time necessary to remove these teachers from the classroom.

Summary

We believe that intentionally leading professional learning is an important responsibility of the principal. Here is where teacher leaders emerge and work at their best. Rather than being tied down with operational concerns, teacher leaders want to learn in order to help others learn and, most important, to ensure that more students learn. Principals can use the Professional Learning Rubric (Figure 6.3) to self-assess professional learning in their schools.

Figure 6.3. Professional Learning Rubric

Quality teacher leadership requires alignment of teacher leadership with professional learning.	
Unsure & Unskilled	Professional learning opportunities are available, but may or may not be related to the school's vision or aligned with individual teacher needs.
Moving Along	A school vision has been developed and decisions regarding professional learning evolve from the vision. Teacher leaders are directly involved in determining what many of these learning opportunities will be.
Leading Teacher Leaders	All professional learning opportunities are aligned with the school's vision and the individuals' job needs; a variety of learning formats are employed for delivery of learning; everyone in the school is involved in continuous learning. Teacher leaders have improved their leadership skills through specific professional learning opportunities.

The knowledge base regarding professional learning is highly developed, and we can no longer ignore what is known about this field. As teachers move into structures for collective learning within a comprehensive professional learning model, teacher leadership will grow. Even reluctant teacher learners must join in, because no student should be taught by a teacher who does not learn.

Resources

6.1 The Northwest Regional Educational Laboratory's Lab National Network website—Site map to access regional educational research and development organizations funded by the U.S. Education Department, Institute of Education Sciences (IES). Retrieved on September 25, 2005, from http://www.nwrel.org/national

6.2 Education Reform website—Site organized around the National Staff Development Council's Standards for Staff Development. Each standard is linked to relevant resources. Retrieved on September 25, 2005, from http://prodev.edreform.net/

6.3 Annenberg Media Learner.org—Video on demand and other resources provided for examining critical issues in school reform, such as *A Community of Learners*. Provides information on critical friends groups, looking at student work, and other practices that engage teachers in collaborative learning. Retrieved on September 25, 2005, from http://www.learner.org/

6.4 Sweeney, D. (2003). *Learning along the way: Professional development by and for teachers.* Portland, ME: Stenhouse—Provides practical suggestion on how to form study groups.

6.5 Jolly, A. (2005). *A facilitator's guide to professional learning teams.* Greensboro, NC: SERVE—Step-by-step process to teacher learning in teams. Retrieved on September 25, 2005, from http://www. serve.org/_downloads/publications/PLTbook sam.pdf

6.6 GoENC.com—Previously known as ENC.com, this website for mathematics and science education was formerly funded by the U.S. Department of Education. Currently, the website is subscriber-based, but it contains excellent information on how to design professional learning. Retrieved on September 25, 2005, from http://www.goenc.com/

6.7 Professional Development: Learning From the Best—Provides a comprehensive toolkit to design professional learning. Retrieved on September 25, 2005, from http://www.ncrel.org/pd/toolkit.htm

6.8 Design Your Professional Development Program—The Association for Supervision and Curriculum Development provides a step-by-step process for designing professional learning. Retrieved on September 25, 2005, from http://webserver3.ascd.org/ossd/planning.html

6.9 Action Research website—Updated links to websites supporting action research. Retrieved on September 25, 2005, from http://www.emtech.net/actionresearch.htm

6.10 Easton, L. B. (2004). *Powerful designs for professional learning.* Oxford, OH: National Staff Development Council. This book contains detailed information on 21 professional learning strategies. For each of the strategies there is a description of its intended purpose, it component parts, and its application. Additionally, forms for each of the learning strategies are on a CD that accompanies the book.

6.11 Teacher Leaders Network. Professional Learning Communities: A List of Resources—Links to numerous resources related to professional learning communities. Retrieved on September 25, 2005, from http://www.teacherleaders.org/Resources/profcomms. html

6.12 Barker, C. L., & Searchwell, C. J. (1998). *Writing meaningful teacher evaluations—right now!!! The principal's quick-start reference guide.* Thousand Oaks, CA: Corwin Press—A how-to guide that addresses specific performance statements and the best vocabulary to use in evaluating teachers.

Tools

Tool 6.1　Assessing Supportive Conditions for Professional Learning

Purpose: To determine perceived and real supportive conditions for professional learning.

Materials: Copies of the charts in Figure 6.4.

Directions: The principal completes the grid below and asks a cross section of teachers to anonymously answer the questions. Compile and compare the results for each question. After all data are collected, invite teachers who answered the question into a conversation about the results.

Figure 6.4. Questions to Assess Supportive Conditions for Professional Learning

Principal's Questions	
1. Do you support teachers in authentically sharing in decision making, or do their suggestions serve as advice to you?	2. Does the school or school system provide adequate financial support for teacher learning?
3. If you asked five teachers at your school, picked randomly, could they articulate what the vision is for the entire school?	4. When teachers are learning, do you learn with them?
5. Are there frequent opportunities for teachers to learn together and apply what they learn?	6. How often do teachers in your school visit each other's classrooms to learn from each other?
Teachers' Questions	
1. When teachers are asked to share in decisions, is there follow through on those decisions, or is the input perceived as advice?	2. Do you feel that teachers are provided adequate resources for professional growth and development?

Teachers' Questions	
3. What is the vision for the entire school?	4. Does the principal of the school attend most professional development sessions with the teachers?
5. Do you frequently participate in professional development and then apply what you have learned?	6. How often do you visit another teacher's classroom to learn from that teacher?

Items adapted from North Carolina's Teacher Working Conditions Survey. The entire survey and reports based on the survey response can be found at the website of the Office of the Governor of the State of North Carolina, http://www.governor.state.nc.us

Tool 6.2 *Inventory of Professional Learning Formats*

Purpose: To determine current professional learning formats used and propose a desired state that may require actions to be taken.

Materials: Copies of the grid in Figure 6.6, adding other formats to the list if they are currently being used or should be considered for use.

Directions:

- Read the items in the column labeled "Formats in Use" and identify whether these formats are currently used by making a mark in the column to the left labeled "Current Reality."

- For each item currently in use, decide whether less of this format is needed, the amount is okay as it is, or more of this format is desirable. Fill in the column labeled "Desired Reality" appropriately.

- In the last column, indicate actions needed for each format in order to move it toward the "Desired Reality."

- Use this information to assist in developing the school improvement plan, particularly as it relates to professional learning opportunities.

Figure 6.6. Inventory of Professional Learning Formats

Current Reality	Formats in Use	Desired Reality	Actions to Be Taken
Used/ Not Used?		Less/OK/ More?	
	Action research		
	Curriculum development		
	Workshops		
	Collaborative lesson planning		
	Study groups		
	Professional networks/ organizations		
	Examination of student work		
	Intensive summer institutes with follow-up		
	Mentoring		
	Professional conferences		
	Coaching		

Tool 6.3   Reluctant Teacher Learners

Use this tool to help you reflect on the staff as a whole regarding behaviors of reluctant teacher learners. An organizational diagnosis using this tool or another device increases your awareness of individual needs that may be influencing the entire school.

Directions:

- Read each behavior and determine the percentage of the teaching staff who exhibit the behavior.
- Review Chapter 6 to determine the types of "Reluctant Teacher Learners" on the staff.
- If one or more "Reluctant Teacher Learner" types make up more than 50 percent of the staff, you may need to repair relationships or confront incompetence before moving forward with this new view of leading and learning.

Behaviors	Percent of Teaching Staff Displaying the Behavior						
Does not work closely with other adults	0	1–10%	11–20%	21–30%	31–40%	41–50%	50%+
Is not interested in trying new programs or strategies	0	1–10%	11–20%	21–30%	31–40%	41–50%	50%+
Uses psychological abuse to control students	0	1–10%	11–20%	21–30%	31–40%	41–50%	50%+
Spends majority of time in his or her own classroom	0	1–10%	11–20%	21–30%	31–40%	41–50%	50%+
Shows evidence of emotional extremes	0	1–10%	11–20%	21–30%	31–40%	41–50%	50%+
Does little teaching when at work; high absenteeism	0	1–10%	11–20%	21–30%	31–40%	41–50%	50%+
Demonstrates a general dislike for most students	0	1–10%	11–20%	21–30%	31–40%	41–50%	50%+
Has been accused of physical abuse of students	0	1–10%	11–20%	21–30%	31–40%	41–50%	50%+

Receives numerous parent complaints	0	1–10%	11–20%	21–30%	31–40%	41–50%	50%+
Rarely socializes with other teachers	0	1–10%	11–20%	21–30%	31–40%	41–50%	50%+
Students in the classroom do not perform well academically	0	1–10%	11–20%	21–30%	31–40%	41–50%	50%+
Has poor self-discipline	0	1–10%	11–20%	21–30%	31–40%	41–50%	50%+
Experiences difficulty with student discipline	0	1–10%	11–20%	21–30%	31–40%	41–50%	50%+
Believes he or she can secure own resources	0	1–10%	11–20%	21–30%	31–40%	41–50%	50%+
Has unacknowledged problems in teaching	0	1–10%	11–20%	21–30%	31–40%	41–50%	50%+

Part 3

Supporting and Sustaining Teacher Leadership

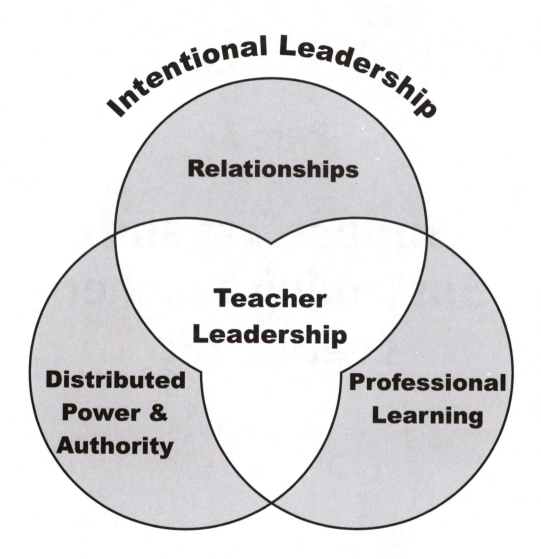

Part 3

Supporting and Sustaining Teacher Leadership

In this part, we return to the Framework for Intentional Leadership model. As the focus moves to continuing the work, it is important to look once again at all the components. If teacher leadership is to be sustained, then intentional leadership must be a continuation of actions to build relationships, distribute power and authority, and align professional learning in order to allow teacher leadership to emerge. In Chapter 7, "Creating a Context of Support for Teacher Leaders," we discuss the foreseeable tensions in the relationships between principals and teacher leaders. While acknowledging that informal leadership can be powerful, we look more closely at formal teacher leader roles. With the increase in formal teacher leadership roles, we believe that principals need strategies to support these teachers. Finally, we recommend leadership development skills teachers need.

An expanded description of Markham Middle School frames Chapter 8, "Sustaining Teacher Leadership." This is followed by commentaries regarding how to sustain support for teacher leading and learning beyond the leadership of a single principal. Then we look at intentional leadership strategies in the larger context, beyond the school where predictable disruptors can cause a school to lose sight of the vision. Finally, we share a letter from Jay, the principal of Markham Middle School, to incumbent and potential principals regarding the work to be done and their role in making it happen.

7

Creating a Context of Support for Teacher Leaders

Building relationships with teacher leaders is not only the first step to providing supportive conditions for them, it is critical to the principal's success and the health of the school culture. A poor relationship with an informal or formal powerful teacher leader may cause the principal stress, but it may also result in mayhem among the staff members. Distributing power and authority is critical in order for teachers to be authentically involved in making decisions and being accountable for results. Finally, aligning teacher leadership with professional learning is the core work of the principal as an instructional leader. The energy and effort put into promoting, building, and sustaining teacher leadership is aimed at improving student learning. If principals expect to reap the full benefits of teacher leadership, they can no longer delegate to teacher leaders without offering leadership development opportunities, coaching them in their work, and securing needed resources.

In the following section, we describe the predictable causes of tension between principals and teacher leaders. Then we describe the various informal and formal teacher leader roles, with emphasis on the emerging formal instructional teacher leader role. Finally, we recommend the areas of skill development that are critical for teacher leader success.

Tensions Between Principals and Teacher Leaders

The ways in which principals interact with teacher leaders will determine the effectiveness of this work. In his study of principal and teacher leader relationships, Anderson (2004) described three models of how these key leaders might work together. First, there is the "buffered principal" (p. 107), who is surrounded by a small group of teacher leaders but is mostly isolated from other teachers. These teacher leaders are viewed by the other teachers as an elitist group that may or may not allow other teachers or even the principal access to information and resources. The second model is "contested" (p. 109), where the teacher leaders hold an unskilled principal hostage in order to maintain the status quo. These teachers feel they are guarding the school against attempts to damage what they believe is good. Finally, there is the "interactive principal" (p. 108), who is inclusive in offering formal and informal leadership opportunities for all teachers based on teachers' interests. Similar to a food buffet, these principals lay out the issues that must be solved and engage teachers who step up and choose freely from the options available. We believe that principals can develop skills and strategies to productively work interactively with teacher leaders.

Both principals and teacher leaders come to their relationships with their own resources and needs. Principals' resources are housed within the formal power and authority of their positions, whereas teacher leaders' resources are more intangible and based on their human and social capital. If principals and teacher leaders are to work together, their relationships must be reciprocal; each must be allowed to tap the resources of the other with the purpose of achieving the shared vision for student learning. Principals and teacher leaders have different needs, interests, and perceived role identities (Smylie & Brownlee-Conyers, 1992). Teacher leaders are concerned about their relationships with their students, colleagues, and the principal. If these relationships are put in danger, the teacher leader cannot work effectively. On the other hand, principals see their needs, interests, and perceived role identities connected to the assignment of tasks, the budget, personnel evaluation, and interactions with external publics. If the principals perceive teacher leaders as impinging on these, they will most likely feel uncertain about how to work with these teachers. The principal's role is to build trust and openness with the teacher leader in order to focus on their joint responsibilities while attending to their uniqueness. In order to build this trust, principals and teacher leaders must feel that the other person is not a threat.

The level of ambiguity in roles is dependent on the quality of the principal–teacher leader relationship. If a teacher assumes a single task and works relatively independent of the principal, there is less tension than when a teacher takes on a formal, full-time instructional leadership role. Both principals and teacher leaders must pay attention to the building of relationships that will move beyond individuals' personal interests to focus on the tasks to be accomplished.

Teacher Leader Functions

Teacher leaders assume their roles through countless pathways. Some emerge to informally take on responsibilities that others do not want or simply do not see as problems. Others are selected, either by the principal or a leadership group, to take on formal managerial or leadership roles, such as department chair. Finally, with school reform initiatives, the number of teacher leaders taking on instructional leadership roles through a directive from either the central office or the school's leadership is increasing.

Ubiquitous Teacher Leadership

Think of informal teacher leadership as a kaleidoscope, with teachers moving in and out of various leadership roles that change frequently depending on need. These teacher leaders often take on responsibilities when they want to use their talents to address a problem they perceive as important. In most cases, they see themselves not as leaders but as people who saw tasks that needed to be done and did them.

Principals who build relationships with informal teacher leaders can set in motion incredible accomplishments, such as establishing procedures for a safe school, designing a tutorial program, or building parent-community programs. There is no limit to the opportunities for informal teacher leaders to take action. In working with teacher leaders, we are amazed at their ideas and dismayed at how often principals fail to take advantage of the willingness and talents of these teachers.

Teams of teachers who are focused on student learning also need the principal's attention. In these teams, informal leadership emerges in the collaborative work of teachers. Teachers take on leadership responsibilities on an as-needed basis. If a team of teachers identifies that their students are struggling with a particular skill, the teachers look to the teacher or teachers who have expertise in this area. Through joint inquiry, teachers discover their strengths, build on them, and provide leadership to the team.

Recognized Teacher Leader Functions

In the operation of most schools there are also formal teacher leaders who assume different leadership roles focused on governance, student activities, managerial or leadership tasks, or primary instructional leadership. The relationships between the principal and these teacher leaders may demand structure that is not necessary with informal teacher leaders.

Governance Leadership Roles

Most schools have site-based governance structures. How elaborate these structures are depends on factors like the size of the school, state and local mandates for shared governance, maturity of the principal and staff in the distribution of power and authority, and the influence of teachers' professional organizations. Membership in governance structures places teachers in formal teacher leadership roles. Whether serving as a member or chair of a site-based leadership team, a behavior intervention council to assist classroom teachers, or a hearing committee where teachers provide a forum for hearing faculty grievances and student appeals, teachers in these roles are formal leaders making decisions. Teacher leaders may also represent their school on governance entities at the school system level, such as systemwide decision-making councils, textbook adoption committees, or other groups that make decisions affecting the school system.

Student Activities Leadership Roles

Another category of essential leadership roles are those focused on cocurricular or extracurricular activities. Teachers accept the formal responsibilities for working with various student activities, including subject-area clubs, team and individual sports, honorary and scholastic organizations, and service clubs. Quite often a teacher serves as a formal coordinator to help an individual group in communicating with other groups, making sure efforts are not being duplicated, securing facilities, coordinating fund-raising activities, and publicizing events. In large high schools, this role may require time released from teaching responsibilities.

Managerial or Leadership Roles

There are countless teacher leaders who take on managerial or leadership roles to keep the school functioning. These roles include positions such as team leader, union representative, mentor, or school improvement team chair. For most of these roles, teacher leaders serve as liaisons between classroom teachers and the administration, representing their team, department, or grade level in discussions about schoolwide issues.

Working with these teacher leaders offers the principal an opportunity to put together a cadre of emissaries to build teacher leadership. Although teachers in these roles handle the administrative tasks related to their jobs, they also interact with the teachers they represent. These people are strategically placed to recognize, initiate, and support informal teacher leaders. Even when a school has a formal instructional teacher leader, that one person cannot work with every member of the staff; therefore, principals rely on team leaders, department chairs, and others to build their teams to improve student learning. It is the principal's task to build relationships with these leaders so that they are skilled and willing to be inclusive in their work with others.

Team leaders and department chairs are increasingly being asked to become instructional leaders. If supportive structures are present, including time, space, and an expectation for collaboration, powerful learning can take place through shared collective learning, joint planning, and personal practice for student learning. Principals should be sensitive to the needs of team leaders. For example, if a teacher leader, who may have previously worked with a well-functioning team, moves into another team with different group dynamics, he or she may face another team that does not work as well together. In this situation, the principal could coach the teacher leader on how to build relationships within the team in order to delegate responsibilities.

Instructional Leadership Roles

Teacher leaders who assume formal instructional leadership roles purposely work with teachers to improve student learning. There is a growing trend to build structures within schools and school systems to select teachers for responsibilities such as staff developer, literacy coach, and lead teacher. Because formal instructional teacher leadership is a relatively new concept, many principals do not have experience in building relationships with a person in this position.

The relationships of principals and teacher leaders depend to a great extent on their previous experience together. If over the years teachers have assumed leadership roles within a school's supportive culture before moving into a more formal role, then the building of a positive relationship will be more rapid; if the school system assigns a new teacher leader to a school, relationship building will take more time. There are certainly other personal factors that will influence this process, some of which we described in Chapter 3.

Principal Support of Instructional Teacher Leaders

Regardless of how teacher leaders assume their roles, their relationship with the principal is an important one. The principal holds power and governs access to resources such as information, opportunities for professional learning, and fiscal support (Vandiver, 1996). Simultaneously, teacher leaders must balance their relationships with their peers. In most situations, even when the relationships are positive, there is still a distinct difference between the principal's role and the teacher leader's role. The principal works with strategic and managerial issues, whereas the teachers focus primarily on teaching and student learning (Crowther et al., 2002).

The following strategies will help principals build strong partnerships with formal teacher instructional leaders:

- Maintain focus on instructional leadership.
- Give access to human and fiscal resources.
- Protect the teacher leader's relationships with peers.
- Collaboratively build and monitor action plans.
- Assist in maintaining balance to avoid overload.
- Be available.

Maintain Focus on Instructional Leadership

From the Field When I took on my job as a reading specialist, I asked to be able to teach a class. For my principal, he was used to having a "third administrator"... but I truly believe the fact that I teach two periods a day makes me credible to my staff. They know my door is always open and they can observe me readily, and they do!

Mary Anne Kosmoski
District Resource Teacher, TLN Member
Tampa, Florida

There is a temptation to ask instructional teacher leaders to take on administrative responsibilities, but by doing this the principal may distract their focus on instructional responsibilities. Emergencies happen in schools, and teacher leaders may, at times, have to pick up duties that are critical to the management operations of the school, but this should not be the norm.

Teacher leader activities that are focused on instructional leadership are varied, but they usually include the following:

- Helping others see how a new approach relates to the shared vision for student learning
- Leading decision making regarding the school's professional learning plan
- Designing and delivering professional learning experiences
- Facilitating groups to examine, design, and use appropriate teaching and learning strategies
- Being available daily to answer questions about teaching and learning
- Mentoring new teachers
- Working with individual teachers who request assistance
- Pulling together assessment data for teachers' use in their decision making

> **From the Field**   I do not consider myself a part of the administration. I am the instructional leader in my building. That's the way the administration refers to me and I refer to myself....It is rare that I perform administrative duties. The reports, plans, etc. that I develop/implement are all based in curriculum or student achievement.
>
> *Christina M. Hunter*, NBCT
> TLN Member
> Greenville, South Carolina

- Seeking outside resources to support teachers
- Building relationships with parents and community members to support student learning
- Working with central office leaders to ensure alignment of school goals with local, state, and national standards
- Advocating beyond the school for policies and resources that support the shared vision for student learning
- Seeking professional renewal for self in order to better serve teachers

Give Access to Human and Fiscal Resources

Leaders cannot function without resources, and teacher leaders are no different. As decisions are made about the teacher leader's responsibilities, principals should identify both human and fiscal resources the teacher will need in their work with other teachers. Individuals responsible for maintaining the budget should be informed about what decision-making power the teacher leader has over any allocated resources. The principal must find ways to give autonomy to teacher leaders in seeking and accessing available resources while maintaining fiscal responsibility.

Protect the Teacher Leader's Relationships with Peers

Most of the teachers who learn and begin to lead believe they are taking on these responsibilities to help their colleagues. Cress and Miller (2003) found in the Teacher Leadership for Systemic Reform Study that these teacher leaders "believe their own kinship with teachers—as teachers themselves—uniquely qualifies them to help. Second, their work is inspired by a sense of moral purpose" (p. 2). Consequently, teacher leaders consider their relationships with their colleagues of utmost importance, yet they are uneasy about them. Although teacher leaders may also have classroom responsibilities, they are taking on roles that are different. They will worry about how they are perceived by other teachers and will go to great lengths to avoid the reprisals that can result when a teacher steps out of the ranks. Even teachers not interested in taking on leadership roles may express resentment that certain teachers are empowered. Formal teacher leader roles are becoming more common, but most school cultures still support the view that all teachers should act and be treated the same.

Many teacher leaders begin with facilitating professional learning activities. These are usually not controversial, and other teachers would expect a person in this role to take on this responsibility. Eventually, as the teacher leader gains confidence and develops trust, he or she can work more intimately with other teachers to improve instruction. The path, though, between where teacher leaders begin and the real work of influencing other teachers is littered with obstacles and the ever-present possibility that other teachers can reject them. Cress and Miller (2003) describe the disadvantages of three strategies teacher leaders may use to build relationships:

1. "Bearing gifts." These gifts, such as materials or other resources, are selected to appeal to other teachers. The disadvantage of this strategy is that once the teachers start receiving the gifts they want them to continue and teacher leaders do not have unlimited resources.

2. "Anything-you-need." The teacher leader may be drawn into the other teachers' agendas rather than promoting the desired instructional improvement.

3. "Unfailing accepting and uncritical language." Not wanting to hurt teachers' feelings, teacher leaders couch their feedback in such a way that the teachers never receive critical feedback. (pp. 3–4)

Helping teacher leaders to understand that these strategies are not productive is part of the coaching role for the principal. One way is to ensure that everyone knows that the principal endorses the work of the teacher leader. The teacher leaders will not be taken seriously by other teachers unless there is a supportive school and culture endorsement from formal leadership, such as the principal, central office leaders, and school district policies. If there is no support, teacher leaders will only work in isolation with individual teachers who agree to learn. Principals need to send the message to all faculty that the teacher leaders' work is important and that other teachers are expected to collaborate.

Most teachers do not see themselves as leaders. When they do move into formal roles, they may feel that they do not have the right to lead colleagues based on their socialization within the teaching culture. Also, they may have agreed to take on these leadership responsibilities because they believe in the effort, but they may still doubt their own knowledge and skills. Although these teachers may have taken on leadership roles in the past, the new role is different: they are not an administrator, and they are not quite the same as the other classroom teachers. This hybrid leadership role can make them feel uneasy.

Predicting these tenuous peer relationships, principals can work to build teacher leaders' confidence through these leadership strategies.

- *Share information.* Teacher leaders need information that will be helpful in problem solving, explaining how to access internal and external information, and offering resources to gather data. If teacher leaders are well informed, they can make better decisions.

- *Start with low-risk tasks that will ensure success.* Principals should recommend starting with assignments that are less threatening, such as meeting with grade-level teams already engaged in conversations about teaching and learning.

- *Celebrate successes, even the small ones.* When principals see the positive results of the teacher leaders' actions, they should find appropriate ways to celebrate the successes. In most cases, this celebration will need to be private because many teacher leaders do not want attention drawn to their efforts, believing it may cause an even broader divide between them and the other teachers.

- *Compliment the teacher leader with specific, behavioral praise.* It is important not only to give praise, but to be specific by referring to what the teacher leader has done. Principals can identify specific behaviors that teacher leaders are carrying out and state how valuable these actions are to the accomplishment of the shared vision.

- *Find opportunities for sharing.* As teacher leaders gain confidence in their work with other teachers, principals should search out opportunities for these teachers to share. Examples of sharing opportunities include presentations to school boards or at professional conferences.

- *Stress the importance of maintaining confidentiality.* When teachers take on these formal roles, they develop a broader perspective of what is happening. At times they will be surprised to find that not all teachers have the same work ethic or commitment that they do. These teacher leaders will be privy to information that should not be shared with others, so the principal and teacher leader must establish an agreement that confidentiality is critical to their success.

Collaboratively Build and Monitor an Action Plan

The school year moves by quickly, and teacher leaders, although well meaning, may not accomplish what they had hoped. To prevent this, the principal and teacher leader should meet to understand the shared vision for the school's instructional needs and agree upon how the teacher leader will take responsibility for responding to these needs. The plan should include short-term goals for the school year and long-term goals that encompass up to five years.

After the plan is developed, regularly scheduled meetings will provide principals and teacher leaders opportunities to keep each other updated on the progress. If the action plan is focused on instructional leadership tasks with measures of accountability, it will be easier for the teacher leader to stay focused and not be distracted by tasks unrelated to his or her primary function.

The principal and the teacher leader should keep each other informed about actions they take. Leaders do not like to be surprised. Finding that a teacher leader has moved in a direction that is not complementary to the overall plan can be a problem; similarly, teacher leaders feel betrayed when principals intercede without communicating with them. Both leaders need autonomy to make decisions, but there must also be constant communication between them to make sure they are moving in the same direction.

Assist in Maintaining Balance to Avoid Overload

See Resource 7.1 Page 183.

See Tool 7.1 Page 186.

Teacher leaders, like principals, can become consumed by serving others. For many teacher leaders, their work is the fulfillment of a desire to leave a legacy by helping others work more effectively with students. In trying to meet this goal, they take on more and more work, frequently resulting in overload that intrudes on their personal lives. Just as the principal must learn to break the bond of dependency, teacher leaders must also. They can learn how to work with other teachers to build independence.

Principals can contribute to teacher leaders' overload. When a teacher leader completes a task well, the tendency is to give this person more tasks. In trying to meet the principal's expectations, the teacher leader will attempt to do everything while gradually falling into a situation that demands too much work in too little time. The traditional principal-teacher relationships in which most teachers are socialized prevent them from refusing this additional work; therefore, principals must protect teacher leaders by monitoring their own reliance on them. Otherwise, teacher leaders will experience stress, become less effective, and possibly move away from leadership roles.

Be Available

This final strategy is difficult for principals because they are pulled in so many directions during the school day. Still, the principal's availability is an important resource for teacher leaders. By regularly putting aside time to talk with teacher leaders, principals can resolve problems and build relationships with them.

Providing support for teacher leaders is important in order to take full advantage of them as resources. As principals and teacher leaders become more comfortable understanding each other's needs and interests, less time is spent on the relationship-building process and more time on the tasks related to instructional leadership.

From the Field   I don't doubt that time is a big factor. But I wonder if there really aren't other issues at play that could be equally contributing to the chaos. Do we really know how to lead? Have any of us been trained how to do that?

Marsha Harding Ratzel, NBCT
Science Teacher, TLN Member
Leawood, Kansas

Teacher Leadership Skills

All informal and formal teacher leaders need support in building specific leadership skills. The assumption that because teachers are confident in leading students, they should know

See
Resource 7.2
Page 183.

how to lead adults is naVve. Principals can coach or find opportunities for teacher leaders to learn how to work with diverse teacher perspectives, make public presentations, and navigate relationships with reticent teachers.

Listed below are several strategies principals can use to help teachers learn how to lead adults:

- Invite teacher leaders to attend institutes or training programs focused on leadership skills.

- Establish a study group to read a current book or articles on leadership.

- Arrange for them to attend conferences where the content will help them as a leaders.

- Invite formal teacher leaders to "shadow" principals through a variety of interactions and, in turn, have principals "shadow" teacher leaders so they can learn each other's roles, provide feedback, and clarify expectations.

- Encourage the central office leaders to establish systemwide networking groups of teacher leaders.

- Debrief difficult experiences to examine other approaches in the future.

- Be open about the principal's own learning about leadership.

See
Resource 7.3
Page 183.

Principals can observe how the teacher leader interacts with others and find ways to help build skills for leading decision making, professional learning, and continuous improvement.

Teacher Leader Skills for Decision Making

Most principals complete a graduate or certification program in order to be licensed as an administrator. Teacher leaders need skills included in these preparation programs, but since they do not wish to pursue administrative licensure, they may not learn them. No assumptions should be made about individuals' proficiency in these skills or their ability to use them in settings outside classrooms. Principals can coach teacher leaders on how to work with others in decision making. For example, if the teacher leader is involved in a project where a far-reaching decision must be made, the principal can advise the teacher to pull together others who will be affected to make the decision rather than deciding alone or with a few close colleagues. Openness when working with others builds relational trust, for both principals and teacher leaders. Principals will need to take on the roles of staff developer and mentor for helping teacher leaders learn these new skills. In fact, principals themselves may discover they need to develop or fine tune some of these leadership skills.

In this section, we describe three categories of skills needed for decision making—meeting leadership, problem solving, and consensus building.

Meeting Leadership

See
Resource 7.4
Page 184.

Much of the operational and developmental work in schools is done through groups of people working together in meetings. Teacher leaders have increased responsibility for organizing and conducting meetings with a variety of colleagues. Woodcock (1989) summarized the work of the meeting leader by stating: "In essence the team leader's role is to ensure that the team has the right blend of roles, that skills are developed, that cooperation and support are maximized and that each individual makes his optimum contribution" (p. 33). Principals can help teacher leaders become aware of actions before, during, and after a meeting that can increase the effectiveness of the group work.

Before the Meeting:

1. *Determine whether or not a meeting is necessary.* Many people claim that at least half or more of the meetings they attend are not necessary because much of what was done or shared could have been done as well or better through other means such as memos, electronic mail, telephone calls, or individual visits. So the first meeting leadership skill is a solid understanding of when a meeting is the best means to use and when other options are better.

2. *Decide the size of the group.* If the intent of the meeting is to have conversation, smaller groups are more likely to meet that purpose. The more people in the group, the less time there is for each person to contribute. Adding individuals to the group can provide benefits by increasing the number of perspectives; on the other hand, it may be less positive because of the decrease in time for each person to talk.

3. *Determine who should attend the meeting.* Perhaps the complaints about meetings are from people who were asked to attend meetings at which they did not really need to be. Determining who should be involved in a decision is important for many reasons, not the least of which is the productive use of time.

4. *Secure an appropriate environment for the meeting.* Everything from the amount of space available, ventilation quality, adequacy of light sources, room temperature, comfort of the furniture, and noise level can influence the actions of participants. Even with limited space in schools, every effort should be made to optimize comfort for meeting participants. The principal can walk through the building with the teacher leader to identify available sites and discuss the merits of each. Teacher leaders should know how to schedule meeting spaces in order to avoid the negative impact of two or more groups using their meeting time trying to determine which group should have the space.

5. *Circulate a draft agenda and request additional agenda items.* Having the agenda in advance of the meeting helps individuals focus their thoughts, gather input from their colleagues, think of additional items to offer, and know what their responsibilities will be. There are many ways to structure a meeting agenda, including the following:
    - Allocate estimated time allotments to each item.
    - Indicate who will be responsible for leading the work on each item.
    - Cluster items so that priority items are not left until the end of the meeting.
    - List topics with annotation and objectives.

In addition, the agenda should not be distributed too early because this may result in it being forgotten or misplaced, whereas sending it too late will create confusion and limited time for individuals to prepare. Receiving the draft agenda five to seven days prior to the meeting usually allows group members time to offer suggestions for revisions and to prepare needed materials.

6. *Prepare meeting room with materials needed before members arrive.* Attention to small details is a sign of caring about the attendees and a time saver. These details might include the following:
    - A sign saying, "Welcome to the Meeting of the…"
    - Name cards for seating arrangements
    - All materials at each participant's seat (pens, pencils, tablets, etc.)
    - Markers for use on chart paper or a dry erase board
    - Refreshments, even if only cool water

During the Meeting

1. *Create group norms for working together.* At the first group meeting, norms should be developed and then revisited and affirmed periodically as the group's work progresses. Group norms are those agreed-upon expectations for the behavior of the group members in their work together. Examples of group norms include "be on time" and "no side conversations." Ideas should be generated by the group members themselves, edited, and finally agreed upon. The norms should be posted at every meeting, referred to when needed to redirect behavior, and reaffirmed and edited periodically to assure their relevance for the group's work.

2. *Identify group member roles.* Specific roles facilitate the efficiency and productivity of a meeting. Among the most common roles are group leader; recorder (who records ideas and captures the minutes); and timekeeper.

3. *Formally bring the meeting to closure.* Even if the entire agenda is not covered, the discussion must finish at the designated ending time. This will avoid stopping in the middle of an important discussion or, perhaps even worse, losing first one member and then another as other obligations require them to leave. The meeting leader needs to monitor time and work to allow for closure to review the following:

   - What was accomplished
   - What was agreed upon, such as who is to complete tasks, under what timeline, between this meeting and the next meeting
   - How well the process went relative to group norms, the agenda structure, or role responsibilities

After the Meeting

1. *Distribute minutes.* All members of the group as well as those who may be affected by decisions, such as the principal, another grade team, or others, should receive a copy of the minutes in either hard copy or an electronic version.

2. *Monitor steps agreed upon.* Based on the tasks and timelines agreed upon during the meeting, the teacher leader should make contact with members of the committee who have responsibilities for actions to determine their progress and provide support if needed.

Problem Solving

Closely related to meeting leadership are skills in problem solving. Many groups are formed with the purpose of dealing with a problem or situation of concern. Teacher leaders usually have excellent problem-solving skills regarding issues in their classrooms, so some of these skills will transfer to their work with adults; others will need to be developed.

According to Ubben and Hughes (1997), "something is a problem when there is a difference between what is currently occurring (the real situation) and what would desirably be happening (ideal situation)" (p. 30). This definition could describe vision development, school improvement planning, or continuous improvement. Teacher leaders need skills in problem solving to achieve the ideal for student learning, program implementation, and policy development. Ubben and Hughes offer the following four criteria to bear in mind when guiding behavior in the area of problem solving:

- *Not all problems are worthy of response.* Principals and teacher leaders need to learn to recognize when a problem is unsolvable or when it will solve itself if left alone.

- *Solutions to small problems may well create larger problems and are therefore better left alone.* An understanding of the complexity and interrelatedness of the various dimensions of a school can help principals and teacher leaders predict the consequences of the suggested actions to address a problem. Doing this can reveal what problems should be addressed and which need to be left alone.

- *Time is necessary to determine to whom the problem belongs and, if necessary, redirect it.* If teachers assumed that all problems in their classrooms are their problem to solve, no other work would get done. Skilled teachers know how to redirect problems and provide support for students to implement appropriate solutions. As teacher leaders increase their work with colleagues, they can use these same skills of questioning, redirecting, and providing support when it comes to problem solving.

- *Determine when it is appropriate to use groups to solve problems and when a unilateral decision is most appropriate.* If there are legal or policy limitations or emergency safety issues that require nonnegotiable actions, any decision will most likely need to be unilateral. Otherwise, involving those affected by a problem and its possible solutions should be the norm. (excerpted from pp. 29–30)

It is helpful for teacher leaders to understand the commonly recommended steps in problem solving. They include the following:

- *Define the problem.* Be sure that there is clarity regarding the issue to

See Resources 7.5, 7.6 Page 184.

be addressed, because "there are few things as useless—if not as dangerous—as the right answer to the wrong question" (Drucker, 1966, p. 353). Time spent making sure that everyone involved in the decision understands the problem will ultimately save time. Too often needless energy is spent working on a symptom rather than on a problem.

- *Establish selection criteria.* The selection criteria should be developed before any discussion begins, preferably immediately after clarifying the problem. By creating the criteria before the generation of alternatives, the criteria will be more objective.

- *Analyze the problem.* In the analysis phase, information is gathered about the situation. Everyone in the group should assist in gathering the information and then hold a discussion to share this information so that members of the group are well informed.

- *Develop alternative solutions.* Once the problem is clear and the analysis is completed, group members can begin to generate possible solutions. While using strategies such as brainstorming and nominal group technique to generate solutions, the meeting leader must ensure that members are not evaluating or discussing alternatives, only generating them.

- *Determine the best solution.* This step of the process requires that selected criteria be applied to each of the alternative solutions generated so that each can be retained for further consideration or discarded if it does not meet the established criteria or cannot be modified to meet them.

- *Assess alternative solutions.* All alternative solutions that meet the criteria must then be assessed for the positive and negative consequences of their implementation and their likely outcome. This work requires the group members to engage in systems thinking in order to produce information that will help the group either select a "best" solution or reject all choices and start over.

- *Implement the solution selected.* Once the solution that appears to have the highest impact and most positive value for the organization is selected, the appropriate actions to make the proposed solution a reality must be taken. This might include changes in areas such as allocation of resources or new behaviors for staff members and students.

- *Evaluate the results.* To continue to improve the quality of the problem-solving process, as well as the quality of decisions, time should be taken to evaluate whether or not the solutions achieved what was intended. Evaluation data may include completed attitude surveys from staff, students, or parents; discipline referrals; student achievement data; or accident reports. These data should relate directly to the comparison of the reality of the situation to the ideal sought. Changes in the process or the approach to the problem should be adjusted based on these results.

Even though the decision maker(s) determined the solution to be "best," others will need to be convinced of that before implementation. For full implementation of identified solutions to occur, there must be advocacy—or at least acceptance—of the recommendations made. When solutions are selected because of law, policy, or safety issues, failure to implement is not an option. However, when the proposed solution is one selected from among several alternatives, agreement by everyone involved must be secured prior to initiation. Teacher leaders must seek to obtain consensus from these individuals. Consensus building is closely associated with problem solving and decision making.

Consensus Building

See Resources 7.7, 7.8 Page 184.

There are three ways to reach a group decision: consensus, compromise, or vote. Consensus occurs when "all members agree to accept a particular solution even though it may not have been their original choice" (Hamilton & Parker, 2001, p. 303). Compromise results when everyone involved has to give up something to enable agreement in the group. Everyone loses something but still gets at least a portion of what they wanted. Voting is used when neither of the other strategies is attainable. Deciding based on a simple majority can leave many people feeling left out or unhappy about the decision. Majority rule is really a political governance process, not a participative decision-making process (Owens, 2001). Voting should be used rarely and only as a last resort.

See Tool 7.2 Page 187.

Consensus building is a participative decision-making process that allows all members a right to be heard. After an open and complete discussion, the group identifies a decision. "If everyone can say, in effect, 'I don't agree with every detail but accept the broad thrust of the decision,' then a consensus has been achieved" (Smith, 2004, p. 119).

We caution principals and teacher leaders that while consensus may be the best process for decision making, it requires trust before it can be fully put into practice. However, even at the early stages of a group's work, the process should be the closest approximation to the ideal as possible. Building consensus takes longer than voting or making a decision unilaterally. Time is needed to make sure that all participants are heard and feel comfortable enough to share concerns aloud without fear. The increase in time for consensus needs to be recognized from the beginning of the decision-making or problem-solving process; if this is unacceptable, another process should be used. Smith (2004) identifies two advantages of consensus in decision making. First, because the group must fully explore every option as a part of the consensus-building process, the decision made is likely to be better than any achieved by the other means. Additionally, when consensus is achieved, the members of the group generally feel more committed to the implementation of the selected solutions.

Teacher Leader Skills to Lead Professional Learning

See
Resource 7.9
Page 184.

Teacher leaders emerge as job-embedded professional learning spreads across the school. Although teacher leaders will be colearners with other teachers, there will be opportunities for them to provide leadership for professional learning. Often teacher leaders are asked to teach other teachers without the support and resources to help them be effective; it is assumed that an outstanding teacher of students will be a good teacher of teachers. It is true that quality professional development should mirror the constructivist teaching that is occurring in classrooms. Yet when teachers take on the role of staff developer or coach, they often forget to use these skills and revert to models they have seen in their own educational experience. Principals can provide teachers with opportunities to build their skills in at least three areas: professional learning design, presentation skills, and coaching.

Professional Learning Design Skills

Teachers may know that the professional learning experiences they had in the past were inadequate, and they may even be able to recognize the reasons. Nevertheless, designing a substantive professional learning experience for other teachers requires skills beyond what many teachers have, so they revert to the traditional workshop design they know. Principals may also lack the skills to design professional learning activities, so their task is to connect teacher leaders with resources to help them.

Listed below are a few strategies for principals to consider:

- Provide resources for teachers to attend regional or national conferences focused on professional learning.

- Invite expert instructional designers from regional service agencies, the central office, or other organizations to coach the teacher leaders.

- Link with school reform efforts where teacher leaders participate in and are taught how to design collaborative learning, such as examination of student work.

- Form teacher leader teams that work together to learn, facilitate, and debrief their experiences in designing and delivering professional learning.

> **From the Field** Many times the professional development programs are also led by our staff…. The facts that "our own" are leading the training, [that] we are able to do it on site, and that there is always follow-up and support available makes our current professional development plan very successful.
>
> *John Vogel*, NBCT
> Mathematics Teacher, TLN Member
> Cape Coral, Florida

Presentation Skills

Teacher leaders are perhaps the best resource for delivering workshops or other professional learning activities. There certainly may be times when a decision is made to bring in an external expert who can help teachers learn specific knowledge and skills, but in most situations, principals can depend on internal teacher leaders. There are few things that feel more risky for teacher leaders than presenting to their colleagues. Principals may need to encourage teacher leaders to present and nurture them as they ease into this stressful territory.

See Resources 7.10, 7.11 Page 184.

The focus of teacher-led workshops can range in complexity from a single information-sharing session to complex skill development. Also, such workshops are only one component of the professional learning. Most of these sessions are just in time, or planned quickly, when the need arises within the workplace.

The principal's roles in helping teachers to design quality presentations for their peers involve the following:

- Modeling quality presentations through professional learning activities facilitated by the principal

- Offering teachers opportunities to learn from other teachers who have a reputation for skillful presentations

- Inviting teachers to participate in local, state, and national organizations that address professional learning

- Meeting with the teacher leaders before presentation sessions to ensure that they have the needed resources

- Debriefing with the teacher leaders after the session to discuss what went well and what they would do differently the next time they present

There are few resources as valuable as teacher leaders who offer to share their knowledge and skills with their peers. When a person who has successfully used a teaching strategy talks to other teachers, they listen.

Coaching

See Resources 7.12, 7.13, 7.14 Page 185–185.

School systems across the country are establishing formal teacher leader roles that include an expectation for coaching other teachers. Whether focused on a school reform effort or a subject area, these teacher leaders are school-based or move from school to school depending on the design of the coaching program. These teachers bring their expertise to other teachers in a variety of venues.

Although teacher leaders have expertise in their area of focus, many lack the skills to coach other teachers, and they quickly learn how difficult it is to move into other teachers' classrooms. If giving feedback to other teachers is an expectation, then many of these "coaches" must learn skills that will help them build trust in order to move beyond the perception by other teachers that their feedback is evaluative.

Teacher leaders who take on the role of coach can be excellent support for principals who establish teaching and learning as their top priority. Teacher leaders provide job-embedded professional development that would be difficult, if not impossible, for an administrator to do. Strategies principals could use to support these teacher leaders include the following:

- Encourage networking with coaches at the local, regional, state, or national level.
- Provide opportunities to attend professional learning experiences that address the skills needed by coaches.
- Be a coach to the teacher leader by modeling listening and questioning skills.
- Help teacher leader coaches understand when to support and when to push teachers to move instructional practice forward.

Writing for Publication

Teacher leaders often find that writing about their practice helps them to reflect on what is happening with their students and how they may change their teaching to better meet students' needs. Encouraging teachers to expand the audience for their writing can help teacher leaders to increase their influence while receiving the satisfaction of publishing their work.

Writing for publication may seem like an overwhelming task for teachers, but there are strategies principals can use to support this effort:

- Link teacher leaders with local university or college teachers who have similar interests. Many teachers in higher education are anxious to be published and look for practitioners who can provide the school-based perspective.

- Provide time for a team of teachers to write collaboratively in a common area of interest.

- Share journal articles that are similar to the type teacher leaders might write.

- Ensure that teacher leaders have access to library databases to provide professional literature to support their writing.

Advocacy Skills

See Resource 7.15 Page 185. There are few educational advocates who are taken as seriously by policymakers as teacher leaders. Unfortunately, teacher leaders often do not see their role as reaching beyond the school to influence policy. Teacher leaders can be encouraged to advocate for what they know is best for students.

It is worth the principal's time to help teachers learn how to advocate effectively. Caution is needed to avoid promoting actions that go against the school system's goals, thereby provoking animosity from principals' supervisors. Strategies may include the following:

- Actively solicit opportunities for teacher leaders to represent the school on systemwide curriculum task groups.

- Invite teacher leaders to attend school board meetings with the principal.

- Engage teacher leaders in conversations with senior-level administrators or policymakers.

- Provide assistance on how to effectively communicate with their legislators about issues of concern.

Summary

In the past, principals who did not understand the potential for teacher leadership simply delegated responsibilities and expected teachers to follow through. In this chapter, we place the responsibility for the success of teacher leaders primarily with the principal; this demands intentional attention to the needs of these teachers. First, principals can recognize the equally powerful potential of teacher leadership in both informal and formal roles. Principals can also build relationships with teacher leaders by offering ongoing support for their unique roles. Finally, there must be explicit consideration for the knowledge and skills that teacher leaders need in order to be effective in their roles.

Over time, the phenomenon of teacher leadership will lose its newness in a school if the principal and teacher leaders have worked to build relationships, distribute power and authority, and align teacher leadership with professional learning. At first, these efforts take an inordinate amount of effort on the part of school leaders, but as teacher leaders take on more responsibilities, the tasks will become less overwhelming. Simultaneously, there should be an intentional plan to sustain teacher leadership over time that is not reliant on the current principal and teacher leaders. The final chapter looks at what actions can be taken to sustain teacher leadership.

Resources

7.1 Brock, B. L., & Grady, M. L. (2002). *Avoiding burnout: A principal's guide to keeping the fire alive.* Thousand Oaks, CA: Corwin—Although this book was written for principals, the strategies suggested are helpful for teacher leaders seeking to find balance in their lives.

7.2 *Leadership Development for Teachers*—This 45-hour blended professional development program includes 18 hours of face-to-face sessions and a 27-hour online component. The program helps teachers learn leadership skills and develop an action plan to address changes needed in their schools. Professional Development Center, phone: (800) 332-2268.

7.3 Miller, B., Moon, J., Elko, S., with Spencer, D. B. (2000). *Teacher leadership in mathematics and science: Casebook and facilitator's guide.* Portsmouth, NH: Heinemann—The authors provide case studies that offer teacher leaders opportunities to examine how dilemmas can be resolved in their leadership roles.

7.4 How to Lead Effective Meetings website—Strategies are provided for leaders of meetings, problems encountered in meetings, and best practices for leaders of meetings. Retrieved on September 25, 2005, from http://www.ohrd.wisc.edu/academicleadershipsupport/howto1.htm

7.5 CreativeMinds.org—This website gives specific directions on how to effectively facilitate brainstorming and brainwriting, as well as other group process strategies. Retrieved on September 25, 2005, from http://creatingminds.org/tools/brainstorming.htm

7.6 Collecting Group Data: Nominal Group Technique—This website lists steps for facilitating a group process technique called the nominal group technique. Retrieved on September 25, 2005, from http://www.uwex.edu/ces/pdande/resources/pdf/Tip sheet3.pdf

7.7 Process Guide #2: Building Consensus—Provides specific guidelines for reaching consensus. Retrieved on September 25, 2005, from http://projects.edtech.sandi.net/staffdev/tpss99/processguides/consensus.html

7.8 Christensen, C., Aaron, S., & Clark, W. (2005). Can schools improve? *Phi Delta Kappan, 86*(7), 545–550—A grid titled "Degrees of Consensus and Tools to Create Agreement" helps readers select the appropriate tool to create agreement in various situations.

7.9 Resources for Teacher Leaders website—Provides assistance for teacher leaders in making presentations, writing for publication, reaching out to the community, mentoring and coaching, providing professional development, and supporting preservice education. Retrieved on September 25, 2005, from http://cse.edc.org/products/teacherleadership/default.asp

7.10 Garmston, R. (1997). *The presenters' fieldbook: A practical guide.* Norwood, MA: Christopher-Gordon Publishers—Topics covered include designing effective presentations, delivering effective presentations, adding "heart and punch" through stories, and working in special situations.

7.11 Kushner, M. (1995). *Successful presentations for dummies.* Forest City, CA: IDG Books—Information on such important issues as establishing credibility, using multimedia techniques, organizing presentations, getting the room right, handling questions, and the 10 biggest mistakes presenters make.

7.12 Neufeld, B., & Roper, D. (2003). *Coaching: A strategy for developing instruction capacity.* Washington, D.C.: The Aspen Institute Program on Education and The Annenberg Institute for School Reform—A 46-page guide to prepare coaches for instructional leadership. Retrieved on September 25, 2005, from http://www.annenberginstitute.org/images/Coaching.pdf

7.13 Teacher Leaders Network. Teacher Coaching and Mentoring: A List of Resources—For teacher leaders who want to improve their skills in coaching and mentoring. Retrieved on September 25, 2005, from http://www.teacherleaders.org/Resources/coaching.html

7.14 The Mentoring Leadership & Resource Network (MLRN)—Website designed to assist mentors of new teachers. Retrieved on September 25, 2005, from http://www.mentors.net/

7.15 ASCD Advocacy Kit—The Association for Supervision and Curriculum Development provides a comprehensive toolkit for teacher leaders who wish to communicate with policymakers, the media, and community leaders. Retrieved on September 25, 2005, from http://www.ascd.org/advocacykit/

Tools

Tool 7.1 *Personal-Professional Balance*

The following are ways that principals can help the teacher leaders in their schools strive for balance in their personal and professional lives:

- Encourage teacher leaders to mark their calendars with appointments for personal activities. Suggest they fill in parts of their calendars with time for other pursuits and not just rely on saying, "I am going to try and attend the walk-a-thon next week." Persuade them to mark it in clearly so that when someone wants some of their time, they can say, "No, I already have an obligation that afternoon."

- Coach teacher leaders in how to delegate leadership opportunities to others. This is difficult for teachers who are trying to balance their relationships with their colleagues. Model effective delegation skills and explicitly share why you are using certain strategies so the teacher leader can learn from you.

- Ask teacher leaders to help you develop potential teacher leaders by establishing a rotation calendar of representation at school activities by other teachers. The teacher leaders do not have to be the only person to represent the team, department, or project.

- Help teacher leaders learn to set specific contact parameters when they are away from the school or in meetings. They may need to learn how to prevent creating a reputation of "the problem solver," which keeps other teachers from doing anything without talking with them first. Share with them that if they find themselves being called multiple times during a meeting, they may have created a level of dependency in their colleagues that needs to be reduced for both the professional health of the colleagues and their own.

- Urge teacher leaders to find one or two activities that they enjoy that are not directly related to education, such as golf, running, volunteering at a hospital, or crafts.

- Recommend that teacher leaders socialize with individuals outside education. For most of us, being in the room with other educators results in "talking shop." We should all try to make sure that on some occasions we have to talk with people who are not educators so that we can hear about their work, their problems, and their perspectives.

- Promote the reading of news magazines and newspapers to get a larger worldview.

- Model balance in your life between your professional and personal pursuits.

Tool 7.2   Building Consensus: Three Techniques
Technique #1: Taking Stock of Where We Are

Adapted from "Consensus," by J. Richardson, Tools for Schools, April/May 2004.

Purpose: To identify the positions or opinions held by every member of the group and determine if concerns exist so that they may be addressed. This activity may be used at several points in the problem-solving/decision-making process, such as when starting discussion on an issue, when monitoring whether the group is moving toward consensus, or when bringing closure to an issue by documenting the consensus achieved.

Materials: Chart from Figure 7.1; dots, sticky notes, or stars

Figure 7.1. Ratings Chart to Build Consensus

10	=	Absolutely yes
9	=	Strongly yes
8	=	Yes
7	=	Somewhat in favor
6	=	Mildly in favor
5	=	Mildly opposed
4	=	Somewhat opposed
3	=	No
2	=	Strongly no
1	=	Absolutely no

Directions:

Step 1: Write the proposed solution or decision. Make sure it is in a place that is visible to every member of the group.

Step 2: Request discussions about the issue. Invite presentation of data, if available.

Step 3: Revisit the proposed solution or decision and reaffirm that this is the issue being considered.

Step 4: Ask that each participant place adhesive dots, sticky notes, or stars on the posted chart next to the rating that best describes how they feel about the proposed solution/decision.

Step 5: Depending on the trust level and positive functioning of the group, information regarding why a particular rating was selected can be voiced openly to the group or written on the sticky notes used to indicate the rating selected. In either case, the purpose for identifying these reasons is to prompt further discussion in the group.

Step 6: Following the discussion of reasons to support or abandon the proposed solution/decision, repeat Step 4. Depending on where the ratings fall, either the choice will be made with consensus or this particular solution/decision will be rejected and a new proposal brought forward.

Technique #2: 5-3-1 Ratings

After solutions that meet the established criteria have been clarified and thoroughly discussed, individuals in the group are given three weighted scores to use: 5, 3, and 1. Each participant places their weighted scores on the solution they feel best addresses the issue in their estimation (5), the next-best solution (3), and the third-best solution (1). Once everyone has placed his or her score, the group eliminates the low-scored items and looks to see if there are any clearly advocated solutions. If there are, each member of the group is asked if he or she can support that particular solution. If there are still members who do not support the solution, or if no clear solution is apparent, additional discussion occurs and the weighted score process is used again.

Technique #3:
You Need Not Be Present to Express Your View

A Delphi or ringi technique can be used without a face-to-face meeting, but meeting leaders need to be aware of time parameters, since both techniques require a significant amount of time to accomplish. Each technique begins with the distribution of a list of solutions to all of the participants. Then proceed as follows:

Delphi Technique

- Ask members to rate all solutions on a scale provided.
- Leader merges all ratings and reissues the document to all group members.
- On the new list is the group members' combined rating for each solution and the individual's rating for each solution. Each group member can compare his or her ratings to those of the group.
- Members are asked to rate each item again, and the process is repeated. Depending on the number of participants, the range of the ratings, and the opportunity for face-to-face discussion, the rounds may continue until a consensus rating is reached or a decision is made to hold a meeting for clarification and discussion before another round of ratings is conducted.

Ringi Technique

- A list of solutions is circulated in a "round robin" fashion among the members.
- Each member rates, critiques, edits, and makes recommendations for the list and then passes it on to the next member, who does the same and then passes it on.
- The document will circulate among the members until a consensus begins to emerge.

8

Sustaining Teacher Leading and Learning

The extent and quality of teacher leadership comes and goes depending on the teachers, the current principal, and the demands of the school system. The only factor principals can control is their leadership behavior; however, most principals hope that after they leave the school, the work they started will continue. Otherwise, why put efforts into bringing about positive educational changes? Most leaders want to leave a tangible legacy from their work, and rather than depending on "hope," effective principals take actions to sustain teacher leadership and, in turn, school improvement efforts that will continue long after their departure.

In this chapter, we return to Markham Middle School as Jay is beginning his last year before retirement. He has served for 12 years as the school's principal. We will see how teacher leadership has evolved in the years since our first visit to MMS in Chapter 2. The entire MMS story serves to identify the intentional actions that Jay and the teachers took to ensure that teacher leading and learning will continue. In addition, there were disrupters that might have caused the school to stray from its intended purposes. We use the most common ones as organizers to offer a few powerful strategies to minimize negative effects of these disrupters and lead to a self-sustaining system. Finally, we offer a few words from Jay as encouragement to current and future principals in their work to promote, build, and sustain teacher leading and learning.

Markham Middle School Revisited

With retirement approaching, Jay walks through the hallways of Markham Middle School (MMS) and remembers the first day of school after his appointment as principal. There were the typical classrooms with bulletin boards and teachers who greeted the students and other teachers in congenial ways. It would be difficult to identify anything wrong from a cursory walk through it, but Jay knew that MMS was not a professional learning community and that the assessment of student learning reflected a lack of teacher leading and learning. Now, as Jay walks around the school during his last "first day of school," he reflects on the various relationships between and among staff members. Their collaboration generates a sense of professionalism and enthusiasm based on teachers working together to improve student learning. During the summer before Jay began his work at MMS, he wrote a personal vision statement setting this level of collaboration as his goal. Jay knows that when he cleans out his top desk drawer on the last day of this school year, he will find his personal vision statement, written and rewritten over the years. It has driven his efforts to push the MMS staff toward a shared vision of high expectations for all students.

During Jay's 12 years at MMS, there has been remarkable progress toward building teacher leadership. Although Jay's vision for a professional learning community was the structure for teacher collaboration, he had a purpose greater than merely bringing teachers together. He saw this structure as a tool for relentlessly pushing for improved pedagogy across all grade levels. Jay saw his responsibility as providing assistance and resources with the expectations that teachers would lead and learn.

During Jay's tenure, instructional approaches changed in response to the changing student population. Each new school year, Jay and the school's teacher leaders collaboratively designed a retreat for the entire staff, at which they could revisit the school's shared vision for student learning. During the retreat, the staff worked together to identify gaps in student learning by analyzing assessment data, examining current teaching strategies, and recommending future teacher learning and related instructional practices. Student data drive decisions about the use of resources, professional learning, and teaching assignments.

Teachers work collaboratively in various groups to tap their strengths. For example, Jaime, who now teaches eighth grade, leads a group of language arts teachers who represent each grade level. This group works to address standards and align curriculum, instruction, and assessment throughout the school. Other groups of teachers work on the same task for other content areas. The management team, responsible for the master schedule, uses input from these content-area teams to make decisions about both student and teacher schedules.

The leadership team has moved from a typical site-based decision-making body to an instructional leadership team. The teacher leaders who serve on this team are considered competent, credible, and approachable by other teachers, so they have not only the power to make decisions, but also the ability to influence the implementation of those decisions. Membership terms on the leadership team are structured so that new members come on each year to replace those current members who are rotating off. Members of this team have emerged as teacher leaders as a result of having been provided professional time to learn and implement successful teaching strategies and then coach other teachers to gain and apply these skills.

With permission from central office leaders, Jay reconfigured the formal leadership team. Instead of two assistant principals, Jay enlisted the help of a teacher leader who was respected by the students to take over the role of handling student discipline. Then he recruited Yolanda, the lead teacher, to take the role of curriculum assistant principal. In this position, Yolanda became the chief executive for teaching and learning. Yolanda collaborates with Theresa, the lead teacher; Leticia, a part-time lead teacher; and members of the leadership team to ensure that the school's vision for student learning is achieved. Additionally, Yolanda, Theresa, and Leticia form a three-member teaching team responsible for three classes each day. Jay is still a member of the leadership team and attends many professional learning activities, but he has delegated the instructional leadership to Yolanda and the other teacher leaders. Teachers know that if Yolanda supports an initiative by attending professional learning activities with them, the decision has Jay's endorsement.

The progress in MMS has not been without conflict. As teachers examined their practice compared to student achievement data, there were often intense conversations about how best to deliver effective instruction. Although teacher individuality was encouraged, Jay was firm about the expectations for collaboration, especially when teachers wanted to revert to the old way of working, such as returning to their classrooms to avoid conflict. Jay continually facilitated the discussions and decision making in ways that brought the focus back on the shared vision for student learning. This took courage and he suffered disappointments, but with perseverance, teachers began to see how working together could make a difference for both the students and themselves. A few teachers were never comfortable that their instructional practices were being publicly examined, so they left the school. New teachers and the teachers who remained worked through tough discussions and learned to collaborate, and as a result, they saw significant student growth.

Professional learning is now job-embedded so that teachers learn while they are using new strategies. Yolanda, Theresa, Leticia, and other teacher leaders present in workshops, model lessons in classrooms, and facilitate team meetings. They are frequently invited to provide feedback while observing other teachers. Breaking the norm of closed and isolated classrooms was one of the most difficult challenges for Jay and the teachers. At first, there were few teachers who purposefully learned from other teachers, but now there are structures in place that provide resources and recognition for all teachers who learn from each other and transfer the new practices to their classrooms.

Teacher leaders no longer see the role of the principal as a job they do not want to pursue. In fact, several teacher leaders from MMS have moved on to principalships in other schools within the system. These new principals are using the same model Jay used at MMS. At central office meetings, Jay often chuckles to himself about how many new principals and central office leaders came from MMS. Now, when conversations are held at the central office principals' meetings, there is a focus on student learning rather than the typical administrative responsibilities. Recently, the current associate superintendent asked Jay to lead a study group for principals focused on resources to help address a new state mandate in reading; there was little hesitation from the principals to participate. A critical mass of principals with a new view of leading is growing within the school system.

Jay did not wait until his last year at MMS to plan for sustaining teacher leading and learning. When he began at MMS, Jay started building relationships with external audiences such as parents, central office leaders, and members of the teachers' organization. Superintendents and other senior-level leaders have changed over the years, but Jay continues to build relationships with the new leaders and share his vision with them. He has repeatedly communicated the importance of sustaining effective school change. Although the next principal has not been selected, teachers, parents, and other staff members have submitted their recommendations for the type of leader needed based on this school's emergence as a mature professional learning community. The current superintendent has developed plans to pilot a process where there will be parent and teacher representatives from the school on the principal selection committee.

Yolanda and other experienced teacher leaders are also building the capacity for continued teacher leadership when they leave the school. Team leaders, lead teachers, and other teachers identify and provide leadership opportunities for potential leaders starting as early as a new teacher's first year of teaching. Their vision is to see the school in a continuous cycle of improvement, no matter who the leaders are. There are no guarantees of success, but Jay and other leaders in MMS are being intentional in their leadership rather than depending on chance to achieve their goal.

Evolution of Teacher Leadership and Learning at MMS

From the start, Jay's purposeful actions to bring teachers together for leading and learning contributed to his plan for leadership succession at MMS. There were specific strategies to build positive relationships, distribute power and authority, and align teacher leadership with teacher learning. Jay also paid attention to the level of support provided for teacher leaders. Throughout the 12 years it took to create the current level of leadership density at MMS, Jay was concurrently preparing the system for the school's self-perpetuation. In this section, we pull strategies from the MMS story.

Building Relationships

When Jay was assigned to MMS, he knew there were both positive and negative social networks, so he took time to assess existing and potential knowledge, skill, and relationship resources in order to increase both human and social capital. Here are strategies that he used:

- Encouraged positive teacher-with-teacher relationships by establishing structures that tapped into existing healthy social networks and available teacher resources
- Invited teams of teachers to participate in external professional learning experiences
- Established teaching schedules based on student needs and linked to existing or potential teacher social networks
- Used traditional meetings, such as faculty meetings, for teacher dialogue and learning
- Set aside his time to learn with the teachers as often as possible
- Matched individual teacher interests with organizational needs and opportunities
- Attended teacher meetings to keep informed and encourage cross-communications
- Followed through on commitments to teachers
- Provided appropriate public and private recognition of teacher leaders
- Taught classes on a regular basis and welcomed observations and feedback
- Learned with the teachers how to manage conflict
- Encouraged teachers who sought new challenges both within and outside the school
- Developed and nurtured relationships with external audiences such as parents, central office personnel, and leaders of the teachers' organization

Distributing Power and Authority

In Jay's previous experience as a principal in other schools, he learned that controlling power and authority only resulted in limited benefits to the school. He came to realize that he could increase power and authority by distributing it to others. These are strategies Jay used to distribute power and authority when he came to MMS:

- Wrote and revisited his personal vision statement describing his goals for achieving improved student learning through teacher leading and learning
- Developed a shared vision for student learning with the faculty and staff
- Maintained control of decision-making authority upon arrival at the school, then gradually distributed this to the leadership team, and then to other teacher leaders
- Established parameters for decision-making authority.
- Restructured and refocused the leadership team so that it became an instructional leadership team
- Made certain that delegated leadership responsibilities were supported with resources and monitored for accountability
- Created structures and operational procedures that assured governance, managerial, instructional, and other leadership opportunities were open to all teachers
- Set up structures so that existing staff led in selecting and inducting new staff
- Ensured that teaching and student placements were driven by student data
- Obtained permission to restructure the traditional administration roles so that teacher leaders had power and authority to focus on student learning and classroom instruction

Aligning Teacher Leadership and Teachers' Professional Learning

To improve student learning at MMS, Jay knew the teachers must be involved in substantive, ongoing professional learning. The purpose of building relationships and distributing power and authority was primarily to establish a school culture in which teachers learned. Strategies Jay used to confront and nurture teachers in their learning included the following:

- Participated with teachers as colearner
- Supported unique, individual teacher learning, but required that most professional learning resources were focused on teacher learning to address student learning needs
- Worked with teacher leaders to set up an evaluation plan of professional learning that reflected student outcomes

- Created job-embedded professional learning with the support of lead teachers and other leaders to work directly with classroom teachers
- Provided resources and held teachers accountable for transferring new instructional strategies
- Used student work as a measure of teaching effectiveness
- Made time available for teachers to share personal practice and learn from others
- Confronted reluctant teacher learners

Support of Teacher Leaders

As Yolanda and others took on formal leadership roles, Jay knew they would need unique types of support to work effectively with their peers. Strategies he used included the following:

- Avoided asking teacher leaders to take on administrative duties
- Provided training and coached teacher leaders in decision-making skills and professional learning skills
- Protected teacher leaders in their relationships with colleagues
- Held teacher leaders accountable for expected outcomes

Markham Middle School and Predictable Disruptors

The Markham Middle School story, if not carefully read, can appear to be an ideal creation, set apart from the realities of the world in which the rest of us live. Not so. MMS experienced the typical external and internal troubles that all schools face—turnover at the system level; teacher attrition; federal, state, and school system mandates; shifting student and community demographics; and now, a change in the principalship. All schools experience such disruptions at one time or another, temporarily taking time and energy from the normal routine. Sadly, dealing with disruptions has become the focus of many school principals, leaving little time or energy to attend to the school's primary mission—teaching and learning. How is it possible that MMS experienced the same disruptions but was able to minimize the negative impacts and remain focused on the school vision? We can assume from the MMS story that there were defensive strategies Jay and the teacher leaders used to prevent these disruptors from becoming distracters from the school's mission. These strategies are described below.

Turnover at Central Office and School Board Levels

When there is a change in the superintendent or key school board members, many principals are hesitant to make major decisions until the new formal leadership is in place. Taking time to wait for this type of direction wastes time at the school level and discourages teacher leaders. Jay maintained support of continuous improvement in spite of these changes by doing the following:

- Sharing the school's vision with central office leaders and continuing to do so even as the individuals in these positions changed
- Creating school system capacity to support the school's vision by nurturing and promoting individuals to assume leadership positions throughout the system
- Teaching and learning with peers and supervisors at every opportunity
- Cultivating strong relationships with parents and others in the school's community

Faculty and Staff Attrition

Faculty and staff members leave schools for various reasons, such as retirement, family moves, or health concerns. These factors are out of the control of principals, so they must plan each year to proactively ensure that replacement faculty and staff members are aligned philosophically with the concept of teachers leading and learning together. Listed here are strategies Jay used to maintain a quality staff:

- Established a strong system led by teachers for recruiting, selecting, inducting, and retaining quality staff members
- Invited current staff to participate in the hiring of new staff members.
- Was explicit during interviews with potential staff members that they would be expected to share their practice, collaborate, and commit to a vision focused on students' learning
- Embedded rituals into the school culture, such as MMS's annual faculty and staff retreat, where everyone recommitted to the school's vision

Shifting Demographics of Students and Community

With increased population diversity in all parts of the country, few schools are untouched by shifting demographics. Most of the MMS teaching staff began their careers working with middle-class, English-speaking students, but then needed to adjust their practice to address more diverse student populations. Here are strategies MMS faculty and staff used to reduce this disruption to the school's mission:

- Established a system for identifying teacher learning needed based on student learning data
- Offered varied approaches to professional learning, relying on expertise from within the school as well as from external sources
- Created structures that required communication focused on sharing practices for effective instruction for all students
- Built strong relationships with parents and other community members, including inviting them to be represented in decision-making structures.

Federal, State, and Local Mandates

Mandates from outside the school are uncontrollable factors that MMS faculty and staff faced. Jay had to effectively communicate these changes to teachers in a positive way so that solutions could be developed without dwelling on what could be perceived as unfair or inappropriate policies. Here are strategies Jay used:

- Established a system of governance structures that can adapt as necessary to accommodate external mandates within existing operations
- Used the school's shared vision as the framework for assessing how mandates can support the focus on student learning
- Kept staff fully informed regarding the mandates, both as they developed and when they were to be implemented
- Invited teachers to assist in determining ways to meet the requirements of the mandates with the least disruption possible to the instructional programming

Changing Principal Leadership

At MMS, the new disruptor is a change in the principalship. However, given the actions that Jay and the teacher leaders took over 12 years, the likelihood of a change in principal disrupting the school's operations is reduced. The system has been created to be self-sustaining; because of this, the new principal at MMS can work with the teachers to continue making improvements. The senior-level leaders must now assume the responsibility for ensuring a good match between the new principal and MMS.

Summary

The importance of sustaining teacher leading and learning while addressing the disruptors that affect all schools will likely become even more imperative as pressures intensify to improve schools. Creating strong systems in a school through building relationships, distributing power and authority, and aligning teacher leadership with professional learning will be the key factors in sustaining that leading and learning and enabling the school's continued improvement.

We realize that schools are in the early phases of putting this new view of leading and learning into practice, and that there are relatively few schools where this is the norm. Still, the proliferation of literature about teacher leadership, teacher leader roles, and interest in sustainability of school improvement encourages us to believe that teacher leadership is expanding, holding the potential for significant changes in schools. Principals who take advantage of this resource can reap the benefits for both themselves and the school. To support this premise, we have asked Jay to close this work in a letter to incumbent and potential principals.

Dear Current and Potential Principals,

If you have read this far, you are very near the end of the book. I have no illusions that you have a fail-safe recipe in your hands that will magically transform you, your school, its staff, its students, and its community into a utopian type of educational Camelot. What you do have is a template that can guide you in developing a school and staff that most surely can become and endure as an authentic community of learners. Take a moment or two and contemplate that as a real possibility.

1. Could it really happen? Absolutely!
2. Can you do it without changing yourself and influencing others to change to greater or lesser degrees? Probably not!
3. Does this book identify the behavioral changes and their concomitant philosophical and psychological orientations that are essential to achieving the desired outcome—the school's vision for student learning? Yes!
4. Are these required changes achievable? Yes!
5. Easily? No!
6. With commitment, perseverance, and patience? Yes!
7. Have any other schools done it? A few have been successful.

Don't hesitate to begin your new adventure. The 21st-century school needs you now—even more so as the years go by. I wish you the very best as you strive to give life to the ideas described in this book.

Sincerely,

Jay

References

Anderson, K. D. (2004). The nature of teacher leadership in schools as reciprocal influences between teacher leaders and principals. *School Effectiveness and School Improvement, 15*(1), 97–113.

Barth, R. S. (2001). *Learning by heart.* San Francisco: Jossey-Bass.

Blasé, J., & Kirby, P. C. (1992). *Bringing out the best in teachers: What effective principals do.* Newbury Park, CA: Corwin Press.

Boles, K., & Troen, V. (2003, September/October). Mamas, don't let your babies grow up to be teachers. *The Harvard Education Letter.*

Bolman, L. G., & Deal, T. E. (2003). *Reframing organizations: Artistry, choice, and leadership* (3rd ed.). San Francisco: Jossey-Bass.

Bridges, E. (1967). A model for shared decision-making in the school principalship. *Educational Administration Quarterly, 3,* 49–61.

Bridges, W. (1991). *Managing transitions: Making the most of change.* Reading, MA: Addison-Wesley.

Bryk, A. S., & Schneider, B. (2002). *Trust in schools: A core resource for improvement.* New York: Russell Sage Foundation.

Coleman, J. S. (1988). Social capital in the creation of human capital. *The American Journal of Sociology, 94, Supplement: Organizations and Institutions: Sociological and Economic Approaches to the Analysis of Social Structure,* 95–120.

Collins, J. (2001). *Good to great: Why some companies make the leap…and others don't.* New York: HarperCollins.

Copland, M. (2001a). *Accelerated Schools Leadership to Learning Conference.* Presentation at Accelerated Schools Leadership to Learning Conference, Storrs, CT.

Copland, M. (2001b). The myth of the superprincipal. *Phi Delta Kappan, 82*(7), 528–532.

Cotton, K. (2003). *Principals and student achievement: What the research says.* Alexandria, VA: Association for Supervision and Curriculum Development.

Cress, K., & Miller, B. (2003). *Understanding limits in teacher leaders' relationships with teachers.* Newton, MA: Education Development Center. Retrieved September 1, 2005, from http://cllc.edc.org/docs/UnderstandingLimitsinRelationships.pdf

Crowther, F., Kaagan, S. S., Ferguson, M., & Hann, L. (2002). *Developing teacher leaders: How teacher leadership enhances school success.* Thousand Oaks, CA: Corwin Press.

Donaldson, G. A. (2001). *Cultivating leadership in schools: Connecting people, purpose, and practice.* New York: Teachers College Press.

Drago-Severson, E. (2004). *Helping teachers learn: Principal leadership for adult growth and development.* Thousand Oaks, CA: Corwin Press.

Drucker, P. F. (1966). *The effective executive.* New York: Harper & Row.

DuFour, R. (2003). Leading edge: 'Collaboration lite' puts student achievement on a starvation diet. *Journal of Staff Development, 24*(3). Retrieved August 9, 2005, from http://www.nsdc.org/library/publications/jsd/dufour244.cfm

Elmore, R. F. (2002). *Bridging the gap between standards and achievement: The imperative for professional development in education.* Washington, DC: Albert Shanker Institute. Retrieved August 9, 2005, from http://www.shankerinstitute.org/Downloads/Bridging_Gap.pdf

Fishbein, S., & Osterman, K. (2000). Crossing over: Learning the roles and rules of the teacher-administrator relationship. Paper presented at the annual meeting of the American Educational Research Association, Seattle. Retrieved March 7, 2005 from http://www.eric.ed.gov/ERICDocs/data/ericdocs2/content_storage_01/0000000b/80/0d/d5/1e.pdf

Fullan, M. (1993). *Change forces: Probing the depths of educational reform.* New York: Falmer Press.

Fullan, M. (2003). *The new meaning of educational change* (3rd ed.). New York: Teachers College Press.

Fullan, M. (2005). *Leadership & sustainability: System thinkers in action.* Thousand Oaks, CA: Corwin Press.

Fullan, M., with Ballew, A. C. (2004). *Leading in a culture of change personal action guide and workbook.* San Francisco: Jossey-Bass.

Garet, M. S., Porter, A. C., Desimone, L., Birman, B. F., & Yoon, K. S. (2001). What makes professional development effective: Results from a national sample of teachers. *American Educational Research Journal, 38*(4), 915–945.

Gonzales, L. D. (2004). *Sustaining teacher leadership: Beyond the boundaries of an enabling school culture.* Lanham, MD: University Press of America.

Goodbread, M. (2000). 'Be friendly, fervent, firm.' *Journal of Staff Development, 21*(3). Retrieved July 31, 2005, from http://www.nsdc.org/library/publications/jsd/voices213.cfm

Hall, G. E., & Hord, S. M. (2001). *Implementing change: Patterns, principles and potholes.* Boston: Allyn & Bacon.

Hamilton, C., with Parker, C. (2001). *Communicating for results: A guide for business and the professions* (6th ed.). Belmont, CA: Wadsworth.

Hargreaves, A., & Fink, D. (2004). The seven principles of sustainable leadership. *Educational Leadership, 61*(7), 8–15.

Heifetz, R. A., & Linsky, M. (2002). *Leadership on the line: Staying alive through the dangers of leading.* Boston: Harvard Business School Press.

Hord, S. M. (Ed.). (2004). *Learning together, leading together: Changing schools through professional learning communities.* New York: Teachers College Press.

Huffman, J. B., & Hipp, K. K. (2003). *Reculturing schools as professional learning communities.* Lanham, MD: Scarecrow Education.

Ingersoll, R. M. (2001). Teacher turnover and teacher shortages: An organizational analysis. *American Educational Research Journal, 38*(3), 499–534.

Ingersoll, R. M., & Smith, T. M. (2003). The wrong solution to the teacher shortage. *Educational Leadership, 60*(8), 30–33.

Institute for Educational Leadership Task Force on Teacher Leadership. (2001). *Leadership for student learning: Redefining the teacher as leader.* Washington, DC: Author. Retrieved July 31, 2005, from http:// www.iel.org/ pubs/sl21ci.html

Joyce, B., & Showers, B. (2002). *Student achievement through staff development* (3rd ed.). Alexandria, VA: Association for Supervision and Curriculum Development.

Joyce, B., Mueller, L., Hrycauk, M., & Hrycauk, W. (2005). Cadres help to create competence: Literacy-oriented school improvement program in Alberta, Canada, boosts teacher leadership and improves abilities. *Journal of Staff Development, 26*(3).

Katzenmeyer, M., & Moller, G. (2001). *Awakening the sleeping giant: Helping teachers develop as leaders* (2nd ed.). Thousand Oaks, CA: Corwin Press.

Kegan, R. (1994). *In over our heads: The mental demands of modern life.* Cambridge, MA: Harvard University Press.

Killion, J. (2002). *What works in the elementary school: Results-based staff development.* Oxford, OH: National Staff Development Council.

Lambert, L. (2002). Toward a deepened theory of constructivist leadership. In L. Lambert, D. Walker, D. P. Zimmerman, J. E. Cooper, M. D. Lambert, M. E. Gardner, & M. Szabo (Eds.), *The Constructivist Leader* (pp. 34–62). New York: Teachers College Press.

Lambert, L. (2003). *Leadership capacity for lasting school improvement.* Alexandria, VA: Association for Supervision and Curriculum Development.

Leeds, D. (2000). *The 7 powers of questions.* New York: Berkley.

Lovely, S. D. (2005). Making the leap to shared leadership. *The Journal of Staff Development, 26*(2), 16–21.

Marshall, K. (2005). It's time to rethink teacher supervision and evaluation. *Phi Delta Kappan, 86*(10), 727–744.

Mid-continent Research for Education & Learning (McREL). (2000). *Principles in action: Stories of award-winning professional development.* Aurora, CO: McREL.

Miller, B., Moon, J., & Elko, S. (2000). *Teacher leadership in mathematics and science.* Portsmouth, NH: Heinemann.

Moller, G., Pankake, A., Huffman, J. B., Hipp, K. A., Cowan, D., & Olivier, D. (2000). *Teacher leadership: A product of supportive and shared leadership within professional learning communities.* Paper presented at the annual meeting of the American Educational Research Association, New Orleans, LA.

National Staff Development Council. (2005). E-X-P-A-N-D-I-N-G your vision of professional development. *The Learning System, 1*(1), 5.

Norton, J. (2004). Today's effective schools have high-capacity leadership. *Working Toward Excellence: The Journal of the Alabama Best Practices Center, 4*(1), 1–2, 8.

Owens, R. G. (2001). *Organizational behavior in education: Instructional leadership and school reform* (7th ed.). Needham Heights, MA: Allyn and Bacon.

Pankake, A. M. (1998). *Implementation: Making things happen.* Larchmont, NY: Eye on Education.

Peterkin, C. (2003). Writing your personal vision/mission statement. Retrieved August 11, 2005 from http:www.eyekai.tv/Articles/writing_your_personal_vision.htm

Phillips-Jones, L. (n.d.). Writing a personal vision statement. Retrieved August 11, 2005, from http://www.mentoringgroup.com/html/articles/mentee_2.html

Platt, A. D., Tripp, C. E., Ogden, W. R., & Fraser, R. G. (2000). *The skillful leader: Confronting mediocre teaching.* Action, MA: Research for Better Teaching.

Quaglia, R. J. (1991). The nature of change. *Journal of Maine Education. 7*(1), 13–16.

Rogers, E. M. (1995). *Diffusion of innovation, 5th Edition.* New York: The Free Press.

Rushfeldt, J. (n.d.). Write powerful mission and vision statements. Retrieved August 11, 2005, from http://www.lifetoolsforwomen.com/p/write-mission-vision.htm

Sanders, W. L. (1998). Value-added assessment. *School Administrator, 55*(11). Retrieved on July 31, 2005, from http://www.aasa.org/publications/sa/1998_12/sanders.htm

Scherer, M. (2002). A soccer game world. *Educational Leadership, 59*(8), 5.

Schlechty, P. (1997). *Inventing better schools.* San Francisco: Jossey-Bass.

Schlechty, P. C. (1993). On the frontier of school reform with trailblazers, pioneers, and settlers. *Journal of Staff Development, 14*(4), 46–51.

Senge, P., Cambron-McCabe, N., Lucas, T., Smith, B., Dutton, J., & Kleiner, A. (2000). *Schools that learn: A fifth discipline fieldbook for educators, parents, and everyone who cares about education.* New York: Doubleday.

Sergiovanni, T. J. (2000). Leadership as stewardship: "Who's serving who?" In Jossey-Bass (Eds.), *The Jossey-Bass reader on educational leadership* (pp. 269–286). San Francisco: Jossey-Bass.

Silva, D. Y., Gimbert, B., & Nolan, J. (2000). Sliding the doors: Locking and unlocking possibilities for teacher leadership. *Teachers College Record, 102*(4), 779–806.

Smith, G. (2004). *Leading the professionals: How to inspire and motivate professional service teams.* Sterling, VA: Kogan Page.

Smith, J. V. (2003). *Key skills for coaching.* Bristol, England: Anaptys Ltd. Retrieved on September 22, 2005, from http://www.uwe.ac.uk/ hsc/learn teach/pec/keycoachingskills.doc

Smylie, M. A., & Brownlee-Conyers, J. (1992). Teacher leaders and their principals: Exploring the development of new working relationships. *Educational Administration Quarterly, 28*(2), 150–184.

Sparks, D. (2005). The final 2%: What it takes to create profound change in leaders. *Journal of Staff Development, 26*(2), 8–15.

Spillane, J. P. (2005). Distributed leadership. *The Educational Forum, 69,* 143–150.

Spillane, J. P., Hallett, T., & Diamond, J. B. (2003). Forms of capital and the construction of leadership: Instructional leadership in urban elementary schools. *Sociology of Education, 76*(1), 1–17.

Spillane, J. P., Halverson, R., & Diamond, J. B. (2004). Towards a theory of leadership practice: A distributed perspective. *Journal of Curriculum Studies, 36*(1), 3–28.

Steffy, B. E., Wolfe, M. P., Pasch, S. H., & Enz, B. J. (Eds.). (1999). *Life cycle of the career teacher.* Thousand Oaks, CA: Corwin Press.

Sykes, G. (1999). Introduction: Teaching as the learning profession. In L. Darling-Hammond & G. Sykes (Eds.), *Teaching as the learning profession: Handbook of policy and practice* (pp. xv–xxiii). San Francisco: Jossey-Bass.

Talbert, J. E., & McLaughlin, M. W. (2002). Professional communities and the artisan model of teaching. *Teachers and teaching: Theory and practice, 8*(3/4), 325–344.

Ubben, G. C., & Hughes, L. W. (1997). *The principal: Creative leadership for effective schools.* Needham Heights, MA: Allyn and Bacon.

Vandiver, F. M. (1996). The identification and characteristics of teacher leaders within a selected elementary school. (Doctoral dissertation, University of Miami, 1996). *Dissertation Abstracts International, 57* (12A), 5122.

Ward, M. E., & Wilcox, B. M. (1999). *Delegation & empowerment.* Larchmont, NY: Eye on Education.

Whitaker, T. (1995). Informal teacher leadership: The key to successful changes in middle level school. *NASSP Bulletin, 79*(567), 76–81.

Whitaker, T. (2002). *Dealing with difficult teachers.* Larchmont, NY: Eye on Education.

Woodcock, M. (1989). *Team development manual* (2nd ed.). Aldershot, England: Gower.

York-Barr, J., & Duke, K. (2004). What do we know about teacher leadership? Findings from two decades of scholarship. *Review of Educational Research, 74*(3), 255–316.

Zinn, L. (1997). *Support and barrier to teacher leadership: Reports of teacher leaders.* Paper presented at the annual meeting of the American Educational Research Association, Chicago.

Index

Drucker, P. F., 177
DuFour, R., 110
Duke, K., 25

E

Economic capital, 68
Egalitarianism myth, 32
Elmore, R. F., 11
Enz, B. J., 45, 50
Expertise, test of, 106
Expert teacher phase, 51
Extracurricular activities, 164

F

Faculty meetings, 78–79
Faculty study groups, 111–112, 143, 172
  142
Federal mandates, 200
Feedback, 109, 168, 181
Ferguson, M., 102
Ferriter, Bill, 86
Fink, D., 35
Flanagan, Nancy, 10
Flexibility, 58
Focus, 58
Formal leadership roles, 26–27, 29–31
  confidentiality and, 170
  governance leadership, 164
  instructional leadership, 165
  managerial roles, 165
  principal delegation of, 55
  student activities leadership, 164
Fraser, R. G., 147
Fullan, M., 25, 41, 42, 75, 128, 141

G

Gap analysis, 140
Garet, M. S., 128
Gimbert, B., 26
Goals, 170
Gonzalez, L. D., 141
Goodbread, M., 35
Governance leadership roles, 164
Graduate study, 88, 132
Graham, Susan, 31
Grogan, Nancy, 128
Group norms, 175
Growth and development, adult, 46

Guthrie, Carolyn, 6

H

Hale, Jessica, 11, 57
Hall, G. E., 41
Hallett, T., 68
Halverson, R., 102
Hamilton, C., 178
Hann, L., 102
Hargreaves, A., 35
Heifetz, R. A., 58, 87, 98, 129
Hipp, K. K., 105
Hiring new staff (procedures), 112
Hord, S. M., 41, 102
Hrycauk, M., 46
Hrycauk, W., 46
Huffman, J. B., 105
Hughes, L. W., 176
Human capital, 68
  new teacher induction and, 113
  seeking information, 70
  self-study, 69–73
  sociogram, 74
  strategies for increasing, 196
  value-added, 73
Hunter, Christina M., 167
Hurtado, Aurora, 79

I

Improvement, sustaining continuous, 35
Incompetent teachers, 147
Individual formal teacher leaders, 30
Induction program, 22–23, 113, 197
Influence, 26, 33
Informal leadership roles, 27, 28, 163
Information, 69–73
  analysis of gathered, 73
  chart of collected, 93
  determining needed, 69–70
  observing and listening for, 72–73
  as resource, 109
  sample areas of, 92
  search documents, 70–71
  sharing, 169
  teacher interviews, to gather, 71–72
Ingersoll, R. M., 33
Initial withdrawal, 52

Parker, C., 178
Pasch, S. H., 45, 50
Pedigo, Michelle, 13, 41, 104
Peer assistance, 146
Peer coaching, 136
Performance appraisal, 146
Persistence, 58
Persistent withdrawal, 52
Personal issues, 53
Personal vision statement, 119–121
Peterkin, C., 119
Phillips-Jones, L., 119
"Pioneers," 48
Platt, A.D., 147
Porter, A. C., 128
Possessive language, 84
Power, authentic distribution of, 10–11, 14, 24, 54–56, 196–197. *See also* Distributing power and authority
Power struggles, 34
Praise, specific behavioral, 169
Presentation skills, 180–181
Principals
 availability of, 82–83, 171
 as coaches, 15
 delegation and, 107
 effective, 6, 9
 expanding duties of, 35–36
 expectations for, 5
 implementation of change and, 58
 as leaders of leaders, 36
 primary responsibility of, 6
 shifting scope of responsibilities, 6–8
 team leaders and, 165
 Principal-with-teacher relationships, 79–86
 accessibility, 82-83
 attending meetings/planning sessions, 80
 attending professional learning activities, 84
 attention to new teachers, 82
 avoiding possessive language, 84
 consistent follow through, 85
 encouraging involvement in school/state/regional projects, 83–84

knowledge of teaching/learning, 79
 matching individuals with opportunities, 83
 providing human/fiscal resources, 82
 questioning/listening skills and, 80–81
 sharing information, 85
 social events, 84–85
 teacher recognition, 86
Problem solving
 behavioral guidance, 176
 recommended steps in, 177-178
Professional associations, 132
Professional development committee, 110–111
Professional development resources, 20–21
Professional learning, 12–13, 15, 21, 24, 127–55
 achieving collective ability, 128–129
 aligning teacher leadership with, 197–198
 assessing supportive conditions for, 151–152
 awards/certification and, 30–31
 collective, 138–139
 comprehensive leading and learning model, 139–141
 design, 134–136, 179–180
 essential on-site program elements, 135
 experiences with, 130–132
 individual efforts at, 30, 132–133
 inventory of professional learning formats, 153
 job-embedded, 194, 198
 options for, 137
 presentation skills, 180–181
 reluctant teacher learners, 144–146, 154–155
 renewal activities, 102
 rubric, 148
 small group/team/partner, 133–134
 teacher expectations for, 128
 teacher leader facilitation of, 168
 teacher learning results, 142–144
 whole-faculty focus, 134